ROCK CAMP

AN ORAL HISTORY: 25 YEARS OF THE
ROCK 'N' ROLL FANTASY CAMP

DAVID FISHOF
WITH TRAVIS ATRIA

Backbeat
Books

Essex, Connecticut

Backbeat
Books

An imprint of Globe Pequot, the trade division of
The Rowman & Littlefield Publishing Group, Inc.
4501 Forbes Blvd., Ste. 200
Lanham, MD 20706
www.rowman.com

Distributed by NATIONAL BOOK NETWORK

Copyright © 2023 by Rock and Roll Fantasy Camp Foundation

Cover Design by Mario Lampic
Illustration by Jesse Vital
Photography by Tom Casey & Tyler Vosburg (Box24 Studio)
Copy Editing by Travis Atria
Interior Layout by Gram Telen

British Library Cataloguing in Publication Information available

Library of Congress Cataloging-in-Publication Data available

ISBN 978-1-4930-7010-7 (cloth : alk. paper)
ISBN 978-1-4930-7011-4 (electronic)

♾™ The paper used in this publication meets the minimum requirements
of American National Standard for Information Sciences—Permanence
of Paper for Printed Library Materials, ANSI/NISO Z39.48-1992

This book was made possible by the Rock and Roll Fantasy Foundation. The foundation was started by a group of RRFC alumni who were interested in using their skills and resources to share the Rock 'n' Roll Fantasy Camp experience with young musicians hoping to start a career in the arts, as well as others who can't afford to attend the camp. Making music is an affirming, lifetime pursuit. It asks for creativity, teamwork, and passion, and in return it provides experiences and relationships that are rewarding, fundamental, and motivating. The purpose and direction of the Rock and Roll Fantasy Foundation is best summed up in its mission statement: Changing lives through music.

This book is dedicated to Pamela Morris, a RRFC stalwart and wife of camper Jeff Morris. Below is a brief message from Jeff in remembrance.

> *September 18, 2011. Pittsburgh, PA.* The two most important things in the Morris household were the Pittsburgh Steelers and music. My wife Pamela and I had just watched the reigning 2010 AFC Champion Steelers soundly defeat the Seattle Seahawks 24–0. Riding high off the win, we now looked for our music fix. We were both vaguely aware of this thing called Rock 'n' Roll Fantasy Camp, and the more we researched and learned about RRFC, the more it seemed a perfect fit. The next camp was in November with Paul Stanley at the Playboy Mansion. Wow! That sounded awesome. And scary.
>
> We were immediately hooked. Pamela and I completely bought into the life-changing powers of the RRFC. The new friends, the experiences, the personal and professional growth opportunities. It all seemed unreal. To capture memories from each of the

camps, Pamela first took tambourines, then vinyl LP records, to collect autographs. There is a wall in my office covered with these containing signatures from the biggest names in the business. But her favorite celebrities of all were the campers. She was a super caring person. She wanted to make everyone feel like a million bucks. She was like the unofficial hostess at camp. She wanted to make sure everyone was comfortable and help new campers navigate the camp. She really loved the idea of the camp, loved the idea of people coming out of their shells, getting out of their comfort zones.

Then our world was rocked, but not in the sense anybody wanted. In 2013, after attending several camps, we learned Pamela had stage IV metastatic cancer. Over the next seven years, she underwent immunotherapy, multiple surgeries, radiation treatments, and countless sleepless nights wondering what tomorrow had in store. Tired and in pain, she never let others see her struggle. She didn't let the disease define her. Most people at camp never knew she was sick. She lived her life as an example of not letting cancer define her. And she never lost her faith or her desire to make others rock stars. It was not uncommon at camp to see Pamela sitting next to a camper and providing words of encouragement.

July 31, 2020. Pittsburgh, PA. At 6:00 a.m., my beautiful bride, who never left an encore un-played, performed her final one on this earth. During her last months, we would reminisce about the rush from that first camp and fondly remember the RRFC family she met and loved over the years. As you turn the pages of this book and read the stories, my wish for you is to sit back, imagine Pamela's smile, and experience and understand what it is like to change lives through music.

We are all Rock Stars.

Jeff Morris

Contents

OPENER

"Rock 'n' roll is the only form of music that has become synonymous with greatness. A politician can be a rockstar. A jet pilot can be a rockstar. If you want to tell someone to do a good job, you say, 'Rock on.' You can't say, 'Country and western on.' There's no other form of music that has that gravitas. The genre itself exemplifies greatness."

—Gene Simmons, KISS.

I'm sitting on my pal's terrace looking directly at the Eden Roc Hotel on Miami Beach and reminiscing about twenty-five years ago, when I hosted my first ever Rock 'n' Roll Fantasy Camp at this very hotel. All these years later, Rob Spiegel, a camper buddy, is about to pick me up in his helicopter to take me to the Key West Film Festival for the premiere of the documentary *Rock Camp: The Movie*, which chronicles the camp's history and many of the people who have participated in it. How crazy the circle comes around: this little idea I had a quarter of a century ago is now a major documentary film.

I think what made the Rock 'n' Roll Fantasy Camp stick around so long is the life-changing effect it has had, both for the campers and for the rock stars. Many rock stars have told me their best friends are the ones they met at camp, and even the biggest stars have shared with me that they see my campers in the front rows of all their arena shows. I explain to them that once a camper has jammed with them on stage, they can't imagine sitting in the nosebleeds, or even ten rows back. They've tasted the dream.

The campers are equally happy because they have made close friendships with the rockers and with their fellow campers. For four days they're hunkered in a rehearsal room with a handful of bandmates they just met and a rock-star mentor, whose goal is to make a roomful of strangers unite and cohere as if they've been playing together their whole lives. The bonding that happens in such a short time is amazing, and that's because the rock camp allows folks to wipe away the years, forget the trials and tribulations of life, and get back to the pure love of music.

One of the great moments at rock camp is the Q-and-A at lunch, where folks get to ask the rock stars anything. And sometimes the rock stars have questions of their own. At the rock camp at Foxwoods Resort Casino in 2014, Joe Perry turned to a camper and asked, "What do you do for a living?" The gentleman responded, "I am a doctor during the week, and on weekends I play in my band and am a guitarist." Joe replied, "You're a guitarist first. You just do that medical stuff to buy guitars." The room burst into applause. That's the spirit of rock camp. The campers are musicians first. They're the type of people, as Joe so keenly observed, who work their jobs to support their true love of music.

When the Covid-19 pandemic hit and concerts and live music had to be abandoned, I turned my focus to take the masterclasses concept from rock camp and transform them on Zoom with hostess Britt Lightning, the lead guitarist of the band Vixen. In only six months, we produced more than 150 nightly classes with rock stars (Roger Daltrey, Alice Cooper, Joe Elliott, Eric Johnson, Styx, the Scorpions), music producers (Mike Clink, Steve Lillywhite, Eddie Kramer), as well as music manager Shep Gordon, and songwriter Desmond Child. I listened every night to these celebrities as they shared the wisdom earned over decades of hard work in the music business, and I realized the common denominator was passion. These artists love their job. They have the same passion the campers have; they just learned how to get over the noise and achieve their goals.

We're living longer these days. There's no reason you can't work until you're eighty, especially if you're doing something you're passionate about. Look at Ringo Starr and Paul McCartney, or Mick Jagger and Keith Richards. That's the promise of rock camp. You never have to lose the passion. So many people wanted to be a musician, or write songs, or be in a cover band, but life got in the way. Rock camp is a place to reset, to open yourself to new possibilities, or to remember old dreams and act on them.

I have seen rock camp change countless lives. One camper was inspired to take his tech knowledge and use it in music. After leaving camp, he founded the website Reverb.com, which allows musicians to sell their instruments globally, and eventually he sold his company to Etsy for $275 million. Another camper became close with his rock-star mentor, Jack Blades, sold his restaurant in Cleveland, and became the tour manager for Blades's band

Night Ranger. One lady came to camp to jam with Slash from Guns N' Roses and didn't tell her boss on Wall Street. She used a sick day and then returned to the office on Monday. But that day, *USA Today* ran an article about the camp, and a photo of her and Slash ended up on the front page. When she returned to work, her boss asked her about it. A week later she resigned and decided she wanted to get into the music business. Or how about the camper who stopped me on the street in Manhattan as I was waiting for my son to meet me for lunch. He said, "Mr. Fishof, wow, I can't believe I'm meeting you here on the street. I just returned from Russia yesterday where my band opened for Aerosmith in Moscow in front of 50,000 screaming fans. It all happened because I met Joe Perry at your camp, and I sent his manager our band's new CD and asked if we could open for Aerosmith because our singer is from Moscow."

In my previous book, *Rock Your Business*, I attempted to share lessons I learned from these amazing rock stars and lessons you might learn from them to help your business succeed. In this book, I decided to let the people who make the camp so great tell the story of what it is and what it does. I hope within these stories you will find inspiration for your life. I hope you will see that it's never too late to change, to rekindle an old dream, or to pursue a new passion. I hope you will believe anything is possible, just as anything was possible for the hundreds of campers who were brave enough to take a chance on their dreams.

Because a rock star is more than just someone who can play a tune or write an album. A rock star is someone who lives his or her dream. A rock star is someone who's leading a life of happiness, pursuing their passion against all odds. And with the right encouragement, and enough courage, anyone can do it.

I'm especially grateful to my pal Raz Ingrasci and his wife Liza, who own the Hoffman Institute (Hoffmaninstitute.org) and showed me I could change my life and create a business I'm passionate about every day, while prioritizing what really matters to me. I'm a lucky family man with my wife Karen, my five children, who are all very successful, and my seven amazing grandchildren (soon to be eight; we have one due in October 2021). Oh, and by the way, *Rock Camp: The Movie* won the Best Music and Arts Film award at the Key West Film Festival, one of the only outdoor live film festivals in 2020. The film became the number-one music documentary on iTunes, currently has a rating of 94 percent on Rotten Tomatoes, and has received rave reviews from the likes of Jimmy Fallon and the *Washington Post*.

Enjoy the book, and never stop dreaming. And catch the film too!

David Fishof

1

BACKSTAGE PASS

I had my first rock 'n' roll fantasies when I was sixteen. They weren't grandiose. I simply wanted to be in my older brother's band. It was perhaps the world's first openly Jewish rock band: the Ruach Revival. "Ruach" is a Hebrew word meaning "spirit." My brother Joey was the leader of the band, the drummer, and my hero. Joey, who is six years older than me, was a natural. He couldn't read music and never took a lesson, but he was a great drummer. The girls loved him, of course. I envied him. I took guitar lessons in hopes of joining his group. But two things made it difficult: one, I had no musical talent; and two, my brother didn't want me in his band. My father, Mark, stepped in as a peacemaker. "David, my son," he said, "instead of being a performer in the band, be the guy who books the band." That's how I began to follow my career path.

I was always a dreamer, the kid who generated ideas and then acted on them. I always knew I wanted to make it big—I never wanted to be anywhere but on top. If I saw something I liked, I went for it. I had launched half a dozen entrepreneurial schemes by the time I graduated high school. A few years after graduation, I was working as a sports agent and I had an idea to put together a baseball camp. I approached my client Lou Piniella of the New York Yankees with the idea, and he loved it. I charged $250 for the week, and Lou and I made more than $10,000 in profits. I never did finish college. I was twenty years old and had a successful business. Isn't that why most people go to college in the first place? I wanted to learn to be a sports agent in school, but now that I had met Lou, I already had the opportunity I needed to start my dream.

When I was twenty years old, I made an appointment with Larry Fleisher, sports agent and president of the NBA Players Association. I wanted to book some of his players at the Catskill Mountain sports camps. Larry introduced me to Earl "The Pearl" Monroe, Celtics great John Havlicek, and others who did a couple camps for me. Earl became a good friend, and through him, I ended up renting an office in New York at 1775 Broadway, where his accountant worked. The first time I went to the office, I discovered that Earl's accountant shared the space with all these amazing rock 'n' roll managers: Shep Gordon (Blondie, Alice Cooper), Gary Kurfirst (the Ramones, Talking Heads, B-52s)— even Madonna's manager was there. Everywhere I looked, there were gold records on the walls. I had always wanted to go into the music business, and seeing the success around me, I longed for that world even more. When reporters would call me to ask about an athlete I represented, I'd tell them my main business was the entertainment business.

After twenty years as a sports agent, I moved into the entertainment business full time. Some people said I was crazy to move away from my incredibly successful career. I had everything, they thought, and now I was about to move into uncharted territory—for what? An idea? But if you want to move from idea to reality, you have to invest in yourself and your idea and be willing to take big risks.

I started my career in the music industry in 1983, and for the next ten years, I continued to work in both industries. I began putting together music tours, including Ringo and his All-Starr Band. I was doing what I loved, having great success, and making great profits. But what really struck me, as I met and mingled with some of the world's great entertainers, was how amazing they were when they were just having fun. It was when they got to let loose and be creative that things were the most exciting. During these years touring with stars, every day I'd get a phone call: What's Ringo like? What's Joe Walsh like? What's Billy Preston like? Everybody wanted to know what it was like to hang out with these rock stars.

I had more than a front-row seat; I was practically in the band. I'll never forget the time Clarence Clemons came to tell me that Levon Helm and Joe Walsh were backstage fighting. "Ringo's the band leader," I told Clarence. "Let him figure it out." A few minutes later, Nils Lofgren came to tell me he was quitting the band. He said there was bloodshed in the dressing room and he didn't want any part of it. That did it. I ran to the dressing room with visions of my tour—and my house—vanishing, and I found

Joe and Levon circling each other, Levon with a smashed bottle in his hand and Joe holding a knife dripping with blood. I was terrified. I didn't know what to do, so I started screaming, "Are you a bunch of babies?" They all broke into uproarious laughter. Then they told me about the prank. Joe and Levon came up with the idea for a fake fight, and everyone pitched in. Joe and Levon sent the tour manager out to buy the props—a rubber knife, fake blood, and a sugar-glass bottle.

When I finally pulled myself together, their laughter ringing in my ears, I had a realization: hey...this is like summer camp, only with rock stars. I started to think, What if I could give these experiences I had on tour with Ringo and his fellow rock stars to others? How incredible would it be to give fans a once-in-a-lifetime opportunity to meet their idols, to jam with them—to live like a rock star?

I loved going on the road. It was like being in the circus. But back home my life was going to shambles. I realized living in a five-story house in Manhattan worth millions of dollars wasn't making me happy. That's when my life changed and I went all in with the camp. Because the only way I know how to do things is to go all in.

But I had good reason to question my decision. The first camp was a terrible financial blow. I never thought I'd do it again, until I was at the Pollstar Live! convention and Tommy Lee, Tommy Shaw, and Sammy Hagar were playing a musical version of *Who Wants to Be a Millionaire*. I wasn't having a good time, and I decided to leave, but as I reached the back of the room, I heard the question: Who created Rock 'n' Roll Fantasy Camp? And Sammy Hagar said, "David Fishof!" I passed Jon Bon Jovi sitting at the bar, and he said, "Fishof, they just mentioned your name!" I walked back into the room, feeling reborn. Right there, I decided to do another camp. Next thing I knew, Eric Sherman, general manager of VH1, called and said, "I want to talk to you about Rock 'n' Roll Fantasy Camp. We love this idea, and we will get behind it." Then came an episode of *The Simpsons*, and a parody on *Saturday Night Live*, and a mention in Jay Leno's monologue on *The Tonight Show*. We ended up doing a series on TLC, as well as a reality TV show on VH1 Classic, produced by Mark Burnett. It just started happening.

Still, it was a bumpy ride. For years, the camp wasn't a success like I was used to having. There were mornings when I couldn't get up. There were mornings when I wondered, "What am I doing this for?" Then I'd open up my emails and someone would say, "Thank you so much. You changed my life." Or I'd get an email from a rock star. Joe Perry wrote and said, "I really enjoyed the camp. It had so much heart to it. It motivated me to finish my project." Something touched me. I had to change. I had to realize that this might not be the biggest business idea right away, but it was changing people's lives.

It took me back to my childhood. My dad was a Holocaust survivor, and he taught me the art of giving. In Victor Frankl's famous book, *Man's Search for Meaning*, he talked about who survived the concentration camps—it was the people that gave, the people that helped others, that shared a piece of bread or a bowl of soup. I remembered my dad doing favors as the cantor in Galveston, Texas, and Brockton, Massachusetts. People would come to him with their problems, and even though he was running all over the place, he always made time to help them. One time I asked him why he worked so hard for others, and he said, "This is what I do. I try to help people." When I saw how rock camp changed lives, I realized I could help people the way my dad did *and* be in rock 'n' roll. It filled my heart with love, with peace, with my true essence. That's what rock camp is all about.

But don't take my word for it. Listen to the people who have taken the ride.

2

CREEN ROOM

Rock camp begins long before the first note is played. My team and I put together our lineup of rock-star counselors—the cream of the crop of touring musicians, who mentor the campers for four days—and special guests, such as Brian Wilson and Roger Daltrey. Sometimes we'll decide on a theme (for instance, the Beatles camp, where campers performed the Sgt. Pepper *album with a horn section and special guest Cheap Trick), and then we take it to the people. As campers begin signing up, we form them into bands, trying to make sure each band has a mixture of skill levels, and then assign the bands to the counselors. Everyone is welcome, no matter their talent level. Some campers come prepared to shred on a guitar like Jeff Beck or pound the drums like John Bonham. Others come having just picked up the bass for the first time or having just started piano lessons. Ultimately, the camp isn't about showing off. It's about learning to come together. It's about reigniting the passion of youth. It's about finding and honoring your true self.*

It takes a lot of work to give the campers this experience. My team puts in hundreds of hours behind the scenes, which the campers never see, just to make the magic happen. I've been lucky to have great people working for me over the years. If you come to camp, I want you to leave all the petty concerns of life behind, forget about where you have to be, and when you have to be there, and what you're going to eat, and the hundred other questions of the day, and focus only on music.

This freedom is crucial, because while the camp draws together people from all walks of life, from tech CEOs, to housewives, to world famous musicians, all the campers want the same thing: an escape from the responsibilities of life and a chance to reconnect with their true passion.

Kelly McPoland (vocalist, office job): I was working in corporate accounts payable, and it was just not what I wanted to be in my life. It was so rigid and cloistered. The camp was my time to be with my people for five days of absolute bliss.

Jeff Morris (guitarist, Microsoft program manager): I'm going on twenty-two years at Microsoft. I was also a musician playing in local cover bands and had made some attempts at going full time, but putting bread on the table and a roof over the head took precedence. I happened to see a rock camp ad pop up on the internet, and it just so happened that the next camp was going to be in Los Angeles at the Playboy Mansion with Paul Stanley. I said, What the hell? I didn't know what I was signing up for, but that was part of the excitement of it.

Jerry Schwartz (guitarist, tattoo artist): I'm probably the typical camper. A guy in his forties who is finally getting his chance to play with his heroes from the 1970s. I started playing guitar when I was about nine years old. When I was a kid growing up we had a band in my basement. Eventually, I had to start working, but the guitar was always there. I never gave up on my passion. Here's what I'll say about rock 'n' roll: if you're thirteen or you're eighty, that feeling when you're at a show and the lights go down, it doesn't change.

Ed Oates (guitarist, co-founder of Oracle): When I retired from Oracle in the mid-'90s, I wanted to start playing more music. For my sixtieth birthday in 2006, my wife wanted to do something nice for me. I had seen an ad for the camp with Brian Wilson, who is one of my heroes and one of the most creative people who ever lived. I was in a band in college with some guys that I still play with now, and my wife decided to send the whole band to rock camp.

Lee Mackson (drummer, attorney): I have no musical ability at all, but I decided I wanted to play an instrument just for fun. I started playing drums, taking lessons locally. I was such a huge Rolling Stones fan, and they had Chuck Leavell at the camp, so I figured it was a perfect chance to go.

Sheerin Moss (vocalist, nurse): Judas Priest is my all-time favorite band, so I decided to do it. My husband said to me, knowing my singing voice, "You're going to sing on stage with Rob Halford? You've got bigger balls than me."

Michelle Capezza (vocalist, attorney): I was diagnosed with cancer. I had surgery and took care of it, but it was still traumatic. It changed my perspective on life and not waiting to do things. Someone told me about the fantasy camp years ago, but I never attended. When I saw the ad for the camp with John Oates, REO Speedwagon, and Steve Ferrone, I said, "Everything is just aligning. It's my time to go."

Peter Gatti (keyboardist, entrepreneur): I was an old rocker from the '80s, but I had not played for many, many years. My wife bought me the camp trip for Father's Day, and although I felt I had "been there, done that," I went with an open mind.

Anthony Mullin (guitarist, clinical psychologist): I was in my third year of my PhD. Rock camp seemed like something fun to do instead of studying and seeing patients. We all love music and at some point probably all shared the same dream. Some of us made it and others didn't, but we're all there for the same reason.

Bruce Hendricks (guitarist, former Disney executive): I had been at Disney as an executive for about twenty-five years. I was taking a sabbatical from work and career, and goofing off, climbing mountains. I had a bucket list of things I wanted to do. I happened to see that Jeff Beck was coming to the camp. I view Jeff as one of the three or four greatest guitar players ever to pick up the instrument. I'm a passionate guitar player, and I play in a band, but I'm not very good. So I was a little nervous about going, and there was a point where I called and tried to cancel. I felt I was not worthy of even standing in Jeff's presence, but they talked me out of it.

Rey More (guitarist, retired senior VP at Motorola): I worked as a senior manager at Motorola, but I *am* a rock guitar player. You do what you do in the context of what you are. My whole career, music imbued my style. I was always a musician, even when I was a manager.

Angie Mariasine (vocalist, investor): I've always loved singing, sometimes did a little karaoke, sang with friends, but that was it. You have kids, you have a life, you have a job, you have to support yourself. Entertainment dreams sort of vanish. Almost seven years ago, I went in for a normal surgery and caught a superbug in the hospital. I had four organ failures. I died twice. I was in a coma for fifteen days. I went through a long recovery. I'm lucky to be alive—I'm actually in a medical journal. I had to relearn how to speak and walk, everything. It was horrendous. I realized that I could have died. Up to this point, there were so many things I wanted to do but had never done, and rock camp was one of them. The camp came to Ontario, and I was in Montreal. I said, The hell with it, let's go.

Jim Stanard (guitarist, insurance agent): I played a lot of music in the '60s and early-'70s, but life got in the way. I got married, got busy with my job, and I stopped playing music. I'd take my guitar out of my closet once a month. About eleven years ago, I was mostly retired, and I decided to take up music again, just to see how I could do. I had time to pursue it. I got some good folks to give me guitar lessons, and I was working pretty hard on it and was fairly happy with how I was progressing. That's when I found the camp.

Troy Garrity (guitarist, private investigator): I don't have a lot of band experience. I'm the guy who goes to open mics with an acoustic guitar. I was looking at it as a venue to learn. I wanted to go play with a band. I just wanted to go play.

Frank Pawlak (guitarist, lawyer): I've had a successful career practicing law in Chicago for close to forty years, and I have spent the last fifteen years or so working in the not-for-profit area, serving currently as general counsel for a not-for-profit organization that provides support services for adults with physical and mental disabilities. But as much as I love practicing law, my first love was always guitar. It is my true passion.

Karen Adams (vocalist, artist): I was a forty-five-year-old wife and mom with two young boys, living in a small town in the mountains of North Carolina. During high school, I was a huge music fan: going to concerts and clubs, often dating musicians. In my twenties, I went to the University of Georgia to achieve my dream of being a visual artist, majoring in painting and drawing. It was an amazing time to be in Athens with the rise of REM and the B-52s. Eventually, I married; then six years later I became a mom. There was little time for music and artwork. That part of me was tucked away indefinitely. Then a friend sent me a link about the camp featuring Roger Daltrey. I have been a huge Who fan since I was fifteen, so in short order, I signed up and began driving to Asheville for voice lessons twice a week. I hadn't sung in public since I was in choir as a kid. Even though I was assured that beginners were welcome, I didn't want to make a fool of myself in front of Roger Daltrey.

Tommy Mullin (vocalist, VP at Seminole Hard Rock Hotel and Casino): A few days before I was getting chickenshit. And the wife says, "You're getting on that plane!" And I'm glad she did. Someone like me, when am I ever gonna have four straight days in a studio jamming like that?

While most campers are adults, many parents attend with their children. The camp has turned out to be especially good at helping parents bond with special needs children.

Larry Harris: I didn't expect a whole lot out of the camp, to be honest. I just wanted to give my daughter something to make her feel better about herself. Helena's dyslexic, ADHD, and dysgraphic. She has a lot of learning disabilities, and she's on medications for it. She used to love singing, but kids at her school picked on her, and she gave it up. Kenny Olson, the guitarist for Kid Rock, encouraged her to sing at the camp, and before I know it, she's on stage singing with Lita Ford. A lot of people just latched onto her there. She's this unique girl who surprises you—she's wearing cat ears, and she gets up onstage and starts playing heavy metal. We still stay in touch with quite a few counselors there. Derek St. Holmes from Ted Nugent was another very caring person. We had an incident at one of the camps. One day, we forgot to give her the medication, and she had a complete meltdown at the rock camp. She started crying, and Derek St. Holmes came out and talked to her. We found out he has a special needs child. He calmed her down and made her feel better while my wife rushed home and got the medicine. Everyone there has been so caring for Helena.

Then there are the rock stars. The first question everyone asks is, How did you get them to come? I have to admit that I got rejected by many of them—and I still do. When I was doing it twenty-five years ago, none of these rock stars wanted to jam with their fans. There weren't meet-and-greets like there are today. The last thing you ever got to see was a rock star. In all my years of touring with Ringo, we never saw the public. I knew that when I heard him sing "With a Little Help from My Friends," I had three minutes to get in the van, because as soon as the song was over, the band would come running off stage, jump in the van, and be gone. Next airport, next city, next show. If I wasn't in the van as the last note was dying out in the arena, they'd leave me behind.

It's the complete opposite with country music, and that's why I've never tried a country fantasy camp. Country musicians are too accessible. They fall in love with their fans. They meet them before the shows and stay late after to meet some more. Rock 'n' roll has an elusiveness to it. Look at all those early videos of the Beatles, and you always see them running away from fans. It's harder to meet a rock star.

But to get the rock stars interested in the camp took time and tenacity. I did everything, including begging and bartering. Steven Tyler heard that I had an extremely rare "Yellow Submarine" jukebox, which I got from Ringo. We made a deal: do the rock camp, and I'll give you the jukebox. I got Steven; he's still got my "Yellow Submarine" jukebox sitting in his kitchen. Other times, I relied on my own chutzpah. I'll never forget the night I saw Slash at the Rock & Roll Hall of Fame, and bought a VIP ticket so I could sit at a table next to him. That was the price of admission, just to hand him my business card and invite him to camp. He came to our tenth anniversary camp in Las Vegas and stayed for twelve hours, jamming an hour with each band. He said to me it was the hardest thing he'd ever done.

Once the word got around, it became easier to get the big names on board. They are a small group, rock stars, and they talk amongst themselves. Many of them kept coming back, because the camp reminded them of what it was like when they first started. Gene Simmons once said to me, "I wish I would have had this when I started so I wouldn't have made as many mistakes." Once the rock stars started buying in, I knew I had something special. Even if you're not making a lot of money, when Roger Daltrey is excited about your project and wants to help—and I couldn't have done the camp without him—you know you're on to something good.

So who are these rock stars? Well, like the campers, they come from different backgrounds and eras, and they have their own reasons for coming to camp.

Paul Stanley (guitarist, vocalist, KISS): I do it selfishly. This isn't a chore. I'm at a point in my life where I don't have to do anything I don't want to do. It's not about money, it's not about perks. I enjoy it. Yesterday, I left the house and said, "I'm going to fantasy camp." Why? Because I want to.

Kane Roberts (guitarist, Alice Cooper): As kids, we have these fantasies, but only the musicians were stupid enough to keep trying to make them come true. But that feeling never goes away, whether you're playing in Wembley or if you end up working at a job going to board meetings. When you're at the camp and you touch the hearts of the campers, you touch the child in each of these campers, you can't help but get an emotional feed off of it. You feel like you did something good.

Teddy Andreadis (keyboardist, Alice Cooper, Guns N' Roses, Chuck Berry): I did it because I saw the people who came to these camps, who were doctors, lawyers, housewives, and at some point in their life, they had that dream of being in a band or being a rock star. So it was up to me to make that little dream of theirs happen.

Adam Kury (bassist, Candlebox): One of the things I looked for personally, selfishly, was to work with other people who have this dream. I've taught lessons over the years, and when you're teaching someone who is really into it, it reminds you of when you were younger and really wanted to learn these things. You feed off of their love of the music and the joy of learning something new.

Max Weinberg (drummer, Bruce Springsteen and the E Street Band): My life has been a fantasy camp. So I know when you get people who played as teenagers and went on to other careers, and then have been able to get together with musicians who they respect, and whose music they listened to, and in many cases learned how to play from listening to that music, it's really a tremendous service. They become rock stars for a weekend.

Tony Franklin (bassist, Whitesnake, Jimmy Page, Kenny Wayne Shepherd): I'm very much into mentoring. It really is a selfless thing. You have to get yourself out of the way. If any of the counselors come in with an ego, that's the wrong attitude. We're there to give the camper an unforgettable experience. I take that very seriously. I have fun in the process, don't get me wrong, but you have to remember why you're there. It was interesting to me to be in a room with such disparate characters, of different situations in life. There are a lot of alpha male CEO types, used to having their own way, and used to calling the shots. And then there are people who are a bit more shy. On one hand, you're trying to suppress the arrogant know-it-alls, and on the other, you're trying to bring out the wallflowers, and make sure everyone has a good time.

Robert "VuDu Man" Sarzo (guitarist, Ozzy Osbourne, Hurricane): Everybody wants a different outcome. Everyone is there for a different reason. I have to figure out why they're there and deliver that. Some people want to have fun playing with the band, other people want to meet the rock stars, others want to perfect their craft. A lot of them are really good players. Maybe they just took that different choice in life. They're still musicians—they just chose another way to make an income. But they still love that feeling of getting in the room, locking that door, and cranking up the amp. I like to try to tap into everybody's feelings so that when they go home, they'll be in a different state of mind and have memories that will last a lifetime. I wish I had something like this when I was young.

Simon Kirke (drummer, Bad Company): One of the things they taught me in rehab was to give back. When I heard about the camp, the opportunity to help other people was too much to pass up. And I loved it. I found out that I like to teach. I like to pass on my knowledge. I bully with charm. That's how I got through to just about everyone I taught. You know, I've been around. I have a few gold albums on the wall. People know of me, and hopefully they respect my work. I think being English helped a little bit.

Joe Perry (guitarist, Aerosmith): We're all fans. There's no room to put on any kind of airs.

Rudy Sarzo (bassist, Quiet Riot, Ozzy Osbourne, Dio): We all start out wanting to be musicians in our teenage years, but life gets in the way. This is an opportunity for the campers to live that dream. Most campers show me photos of themselves as teenagers; they have hair down to their waists. That's who they are, even though they've become heads of medical companies or lawyers. This is a break for them. It's time to live the dream.

Alice Cooper (vocalist): Everybody wants to get better at what they do. I always think the people who show up at the fantasy camp are people who have it in the back of their mind: "You know, this could develop into something." It's good to keep that hope that something can happen if you get really good.

Kip Winger (multi-instrumentalist, Alice Cooper, Winger): It's a great thing for your head to hang around with people who are doing music and learning. The best way to learn is to teach. Everybody is learning and teaching and encouraging. There's very rarely bad vibes. If you have an ego, go home.

Gene Simmons (bassist, KISS): When you see the faces of the younger fans who come, or corporate guys who are stuck in their nine-to-five jobs, they get a chance to climb up to the top level of Mount Olympus and breathe that rarefied air where very few people have ever ascended to become rock gods. Even if that feeling only lasts a day, it's a lifetime memory.

MAKING THE BAND

The next question everyone always asks is, How do you put the bands together? We've tried many things. At first, we held auditions. The campers were told to learn two or three songs, and on the first day, they'd get up and play them for the rock-star counselors. I loved this idea because the campers would get the fantasy experience right away. First thing in the door, and they're playing a Bad Company song to Simon Kirke. But there was a problem with this setup: it was too intimidating. The campers needed more time to acclimate to the brave new world they had just entered.

For the last few years, we have arranged the campers into bands before they arrive and put them in touch with each other and with their rock-star counselor to hack out a basic list of songs they want to learn. I make sure to choose counselors who can meet each player at his or her level, and we work hard to form the bands so that there is a combination of players, from beginners, to intermediates, to experts. Some counselors make special requests. Alan White of Yes said, "Make sure you give me a band that is just great musicians," because Yes music requires technical virtuosity. And then there's guys like Spike Edney, Teddy Andreadis, and Rudy Sarzo, who say to me, "Give me the beginners, and I'll turn them into the best band." I'm happy to oblige.

It works best for the campers this way. When they arrive, they ease into the camp. These days, everybody meets on Zoom before the camp even begins, and they can attend masterclasses with the rock stars in advance. At the camp, there are jam rooms where they can shake off the rust and feel each other out, and there are more masterclasses where the rock stars dispense wisdom, share stories, and give the campers their first taste of the magic: they're more than fans here; they're fellow musicians.

Sammy Hagar (vocalist, Van Halen): The chemistry changes every time. You throw an old guy in there who can play, the chemistry changes. You put a person who just started playing, the chemistry changes. Inspiration is the key. When I'm around these enthusiastic people, I get inspired.

Rudy Sarzo: You never know until you get there how good they are. They might say, "I've been playing for twenty years." Well, maybe they bought the guitar twenty years ago, played it for a week and put it in a closet. So you've owned a guitar for twenty years. Once you're in the room together, you can tell what the strengths and weaknesses are within the first ten minutes. At first, I concentrate on the strengths. Then later I go over the weaknesses, because everybody deserves the same attention at the camp. My philosophy is, don't leave anybody behind. Like a war.

Liam Gowing (multi-instrumentalist, reporter): It's trial by fire. You get put in a group of complete strangers who will form a bond personally and musically, and at the end of the camp have a pretty tight musical thing happening.

Kim Thayil singing with a camper at Seattle Sound Rock Camp.

Bruce Kulick (guitarist, vocalist, Grand Funk Railroad): I got the reputation of being one of the toughest counselors. I wanted these guys to become cohesive and really rise to the occasion at the performance. And the only way to do that is that everybody should be committed. There shouldn't be a weak link, and that means that the person that struggles the most should be lifted up by everybody else.

Sometimes that's easier said than done. I'll never forget the time we had a band whose bass player was in a wheelchair, and he had just begun playing his instrument. The band was unhappy with him and began to complain: "I didn't pay all this money to play with a bass player who can't play!" and "We sounded terrible." Their counselor, Spike Edney, said, "Listen, that's what the rock camp is about. It's about coming together as a band and supporting everybody. The weaker person gets supported by the stronger person." One guy picked himself up and went home. Another guy, who happened to have just sold Napster, invited the band to a party at his house, and they became great friends.

Spike was right. The camp is about coming together, supporting each other, making the whole greater than the sum of its parts. I love that the counselors really get that. For example, if Kip Winger has a band with a weak bass player, and they're not quite ready for the big concert on the final night, he'll go to Rudy Sarzo and say, "Will you help my bass player?" And of course Rudy will do it.

4

THE CAMP

Every camp is different, but the average camp lasts four days. At these camps, the counselors form bands with the campers and rehearse with them, preparing to meet and perform with the special guest in the middle of the week, and then getting ready for the big show on the final day, always at a major venue like the Whisky a Go Go or the House of Blues.

The first day of camp is always the hardest because the campers are scared. They quickly learn that it's one thing to go see Roger Daltrey in concert and have a beer in your hand and reminisce about those songs and how they made you feel when you were young; it's another thing entirely to actually get on stage and play with him. But I want to throw them in the fire. The quicker I can get them in a room jamming with counselors, the easier it'll be. That's why I open up rehearsal rooms on the first day—maybe we'll have a blues room, a Cream room, or a KISS room, and I'll tell the counselors to go in there just to loosen people up. Nerves are taut, expectations are high. Like the first day of summer camp as a kid, the campers are sizing each other up, figuring out where they fit. All the while, they're meeting and jamming with rock 'n' roll icons. At the end of the first day we put on a counselors' jam so the campers can see what it's supposed to look and sound like.

DAY 1

"NERVOUS AS SHIT"

Rey More: You go in and you're nervous as shit.

Troy Garrity: You're wondering, Can I do this? Am I good enough? But you have to do it. There's a lot of forced letting go. They're not messing around. These are professional musicians, and they're going to get you to the point of being ready to perform without a hitch.

Karen Adams: I was totally scared shitless. I had never been on stage before with a band. I didn't want to fuck up. Any little downtime we had, I used to try to memorize lyrics.

Taft Stricklin (guitarist, entrepreneur): You show up and you feel shy. It's like, "How bad am I going to be?" The intimidation of knowing the stars that are going to be there, the bands, the egos—the whole musician thing. I was so nervous walking down the steps to the rehearsal studios. I tuned my guitar four times to make sure it was right. God forbid, I strum and play a wrong note.

Scott Hamilton (drummer, Olympic figure skater): I was a rank beginner. My band was supposed to play "Ticket to Ride" the first night at a cocktail party, but I didn't even know how to start the song. I was so nervous. The very first note, I hit the drums, and both sticks flew out of my hands. I figured, that's the worst that can happen. It can only go up from here.

Anthony Mullin: The first day is apprehension, a good kind of apprehension.

Angie Mariasine: It's like a rollercoaster. You're feeling each other out. I've had amazing bands, I've had horrible bands that turned out to be good.

Karen Adams: It was very much like the first day at any camp when you're a kid. You don't know anybody. There's all this shit going on that's different from your everyday world. You're just kind of standing there with your mouth open, and you just kind of go with the flow. It was action packed. There was no free time.

Miles Schuman (bassist, college student): Within ten minutes of walking through the door, you're in a room jamming with a rock star.

Greg Deal (drummer, former CEO of NAU Country Insurance Company): They expect you to tear into the songs. We'll have breakfast and then we're working right away until lunch time. Then we come back in the afternoon and work some more. We might have a Q-and-A with one of the stars for an hour or so, then you're right back into the room until it's time to break for dinner. Then at night they'll have a jam session. It's a full day of music. Every day is the same. You're rehearsing the songs over and over and over again until you have them just nailed.

Tommy Mullin: They put the musicians in different rooms, and you can go in and jam with them. When you're jamming with Tony Franklin and Brian Tichy, it gets no better than that. That's never gonna happen again. You have to pinch yourself. Did that happen? And they're going, "Let's do another one! That was good!"

Jack Blades (bassist, Night Ranger): We gave a list of like ten songs that they could choose to play, like "Takin' Care of Business" and "Proud Mary," or "Born to Be Wild." You know what I mean? It's almost in your collective consciousness in your brain. And what was great was some guys were so afraid to do it, so I jumped up and got on guitar or bass, and I played with them to give them some encouragement, you know? They're not alone. I love that. And that was the first day! From that point on, it was just excitement, excitement, excitement for everyone.

Ed Oates: We have to get to know each other as people and as musicians. We have to find a song that we all know, that everyone can play, even the least experienced person. Some people are sitting in the back afraid to play a single note, and some people are showing off. The counselor's job is like a schoolteacher—take the kids out of the corner and get them involved. Then they figure out, "What can this band really do? Can they do 'A Day in the Life,' or should they do 'Louie Louie?'"

Kamesh Nagarajan (guitarist, financial advisor): The first day I got in, we went to audition for the counselors. The song was "Proud Mary." And so I'm learning the chords really quick and Jack Blades comes behind me and does one of those '80s things where the guitar, you kind of like jam the guitars together. That moment was almost orgasmic. It felt like every '80s-era MTV video you ever saw.

David James Smith (journalist, tambourinist): You had all these very ordinary people like me, nervous at the attention, slightly overawed to be in the company of these great musicians. You get assigned to a band counselor, and we were given Spencer Davis of the Spencer Davis Group. He had some great stories. He had been invited to Paul McCartney's house to listen to the first pressing of *Sgt. Pepper*, and Paul opened the door with a big spliff in his hand and said, "Step over the dog shit." Whether they were multimillionaires—as many people at this camp were—or they saved for years to go, they were all huge fans of music. They just wanted to get to rub shoulders with these musicians they've loved all their lives. They wanted to film them, they wanted to call their wives or girlfriends and say, "You'll never guess what I've just done." Everyone was absolutely loving it. I was seduced. I'm a cynical Londoner. I thought I was going to be with all these overweight Americans whose judgement has gone AWOL somewhere, but actually they were just really nice people. They were willing to make themselves vulnerable.

I understand why people are so nervous coming to rock camp. I was once invited to go to Michael Jordan's basketball fantasy camp, and I chickened out. I said, "I'm not going to play Michael Jordan like an idiot!" This is where the counselors step in—their job is to take these balls of nerves and turn them into rock stars.

Simon Kirke: You've got to remember, these people are nervous. The first day, they'll play too fast, they may be out of tune. They're a bag of nerves. The first thing to do is to calm them down and teach them something simple. Usually the first thing I'd do, I'd ask them to play me something for thirty or forty seconds, whether it's drums or guitar. I taught both, but mainly drums. Nine times out of ten, they'd rush through, breathless. By the end they'd be winded. I'd say, "Now we got that out of the way, this is how I think we should do it."

Adam Kury: Some of these guys, it's been twenty years since they've played. The biggest thing is getting their confidence back up. We all have insecurities about ourselves as musicians—that never goes away. The counselor has to find what they can do and bring it out of them. This is supposed to be fun. You don't want it to become drudgery.

Jeff Scott Soto (vocalist, SOTO, Trans-Siberian Orchestra, Journey): The first day, you meet your people. My senses are tingling. I'm watching every musician as they're setting up, as they're tuning. You get the levels of where each player is at. You can tell by the way they're holding the sticks, holding the guitar how experienced they are. I start to identify my leaders, who can play what, how advanced or not advanced they are. From there, we have a list of songs to learn, as well as a list of songs to choose from for our special guest. I just want to make sure everybody feels confident. You can play those songs until you're blue in the face, but when your idol walks in the room, it all goes out the window. I want to make sure they can perform these songs backward and forward, so that when the nerves kick in, they can go on autopilot. I want them to walk away with the experience that they did everything they could do when they finally get to play with their heroes. I want to give the campers the experience of a lifetime.

Spike Edney: You notice the looks of terror on the newbies. It's a leveler. But even somebody who does little more than play a tambourine can add something to a band. As a counselor, I try to instill the fear of God in them. *Don't let me down.* Once you find the personality types, you find out how far you can push them before they collapse or crack. Normally, when you push them, they respond.

Rudy Sarzo: The first time I walked into the rehearsal room with the campers, it sounded like a cacophony. But I saw their faces, how joyful they were, how much fun they were having, and that's what was really missing in my life professionally. Reconnecting myself with the original joy I used to have when I was at the musical level of the campers, it was a jolt. It was a realization: this is what I got into music for. That has been at the core of the reason why I do the camp—to reconnect with why I originally started playing, which is about the joy of making music.

Joe Perry: The first thing is to make people feel comfortable and relax, let our hair down, let their guard down. Maybe after a couple of hours they'll realize, "Hey, he's just like me, farther down the road."

Paul Stanley: You're not here to be judged. You're not here to be graded. The person who plays great isn't having any more fun than the person who can barely play. This is recess, man. You're just having a great time. You're here to enjoy yourself.

Meat Loaf (vocalist): I tried to explain to them, don't be nervous because I'm here. Most likely there's some guy down the street working on a phone pole—I'm no different than he is. I just have a different job. I tried to put them at ease so we could talk, so we could communicate. I wanted them to know, I'm no different than you are, except you probably play guitar better than I do. But I can teach you how to improve.

Sammy Hagar: I'm not here as a celebrity. I'm here as a musician. Little by little, it gets to the point where they see I'm a real guy. I can hit a bad note, same as they can. That's why you have to do this thing for a week. It takes getting over all the "goo-goo, ga-ga" and getting down to, "We're musicians, and this is what we do."

Mark Farner (vocalist, lead guitarist, Grand Funk Railroad): They find out that you, too, burp and fart. You're a real person. They go, "You're way different than I imagined, but way better."

Roger Daltrey (vocalist, The Who): When you meet these people for the first time, they're a bit stiff. Once you start playing, even if you can't play very well, music seems to break down the barriers. It's all about just having fun. No one cares about the bum notes.

Max Weinberg: People get outside themselves and they're fourteen years old again. It's all about fun. It's about energy and the feeling you get when you hit a drum really hard, or you play that big power chord on a guitar. It's very elemental, and it keeps you in touch with the essence of being a kid. All of us who play rock 'n' roll for a living, there is definitely a degree of Peter Pan in us all, and I think that's a good thing. It keeps you young at heart. It's never too late to rock and roll.

Tony Franklin: As a counselor, you have to crack the whip, but you also have to be a cheerleader, a producer, and a coach.

Robert Sarzo: I like to let my bands jam. I want it to be spiritual. I don't want them thinking about the song when they get on stage. I want them to get in there and just *feel* it.

Kip Winger: I try to enlighten people on what the miracle of music really is. It's not just jamming on a bunch of songs. It's a highly telepathic, empathetic, emotional experience that can expand your consciousness.

Kane Roberts: My concern is not the skill level. We're going to put something together no matter what. I want them to feel relaxed enough to express themselves and speak up while we're rehearsing if they need anything, and when it comes time to perform, to make them comfortable so they don't freeze up. I like to rehearse as much as possible. I'll say, "I just want the bass and drums to play the song." I'll focus on specific musicians and make them play by themselves. Whatever it takes to get them in the space of performing. At the end of the day, they know these songs forward and backward.

Rudy Sarzo: The first camp I did, our singer was a lawyer whose wife brought him to camp as an anniversary present. It was a surprise. He had never sung before. I approached him and said, "You're a lawyer, so you go in front of a judge and present a case. Let's get you a legal pad. And we're going to write the lyrics to 'Come Together,'" which Steven Tyler had approved as one of the songs he would sing, "and you're going to deliver these lyrics like you're in court." He said, "Okay, I can do that." A couple of days later, when Steven Tyler came into the room to sing those lyrics with the lawyer-singer, who had never done that before, I couldn't wait to see what happened. I thought he's either going to lose his shit, or it's going to be a phenomenal experience. This guy was so focused. Steven was getting in his face and sharing the microphone. It was such a cool moment. By the end of the week, we got to play at the Whisky, and he did it again in front of an audience now. In front of his family, he's singing with Steven Tyler.

And when it works, it's magic.

Bruce Hendricks: I remember standing up there, me and two other guitar players, and we didn't sound so good, and all of a sudden, the drums just came in like thunder, and the whole atmosphere on stage changed. We were like rock stars. I turned around to look, and Danny Seraphine from Chicago had joined us on drums. Chicago was one of my favorite bands, especially early Chicago, and I thought he was one of the great rock drummers of all time. I remember thinking, "Oh my God, we sound amazing." He had a big grin on his face, and he was just layin' it down. Everybody on stage could feel it. We just went to the next level. I was in the presence of greatness. I was on a high the rest of the day.

Taft Stricklin: You come in, have the fantasy experience, and then your feet are in the fire. We had an hour and a half to rehearse and then it's like, "You're going to the Gibson Showroom in Beverly Hills to play a set with a band you just met. Here's a drink to calm your nerves." But leaving the Gibson Showroom, I thought, "Today couldn't have been better." Almost a decade later, I have goosebumps on my arms.

INTERLUDE: THE PLAYBOY MANSION

Sometimes we host a camp in a special location. We've done Abbey Road in London and a camp at Atlantis in the Bahamas. But perhaps the most memorable special-location camp was at the Playboy Mansion. Here's how that happened. Mancow Muller, the famous Chicago radio DJ, used to come to all the camps. "I'm a huge fan of these artists," he told me, "but I never get to see them or speak to them for more than two seconds on my show, and here I get a chance to come hang out with them." One day he showed up with Kevin Burns, the producer of Hugh Hefner's *The Girls Next Door*, and he said, "Come on, David, let's go up to the Playboy Mansion for dinner."

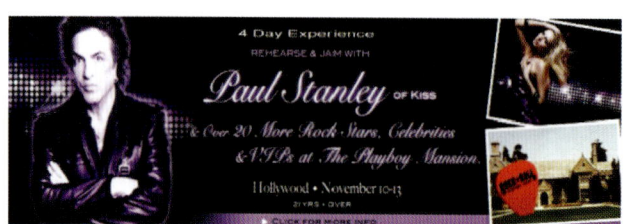

Now I'm in the car sweating. Do I tell my wife I'm going to the Playboy Mansion? I basically got hijacked by Mancow to go, but I don't know if my wife will believe it. Before I could decide what to do, we arrived at Hef's. Now I started to get excited. I couldn't wait to see all the beautiful Bunnies up close and personal. But when I got to the dinner table, I was sitting next to Larry Storch, the comedian from *F Troop*, a couple from Israel, and Tim Hauser, the guy who started the Manhattan Transfer. I felt like I was back in the Catskills, surrounded by all these old people. Perhaps I was better off without the Bunnies distracting me, because during the dinner a great idea struck me: What if I did a camp at the Playboy Mansion? How cool would that be? So I contacted the mansion, rented it out, and booked Paul Stanley as the special guest.

Fast forward: a week before the camp, it was sold out. I visited Hank Fawcett, the manager of the Playboy Mansion, to discuss the menu for the camp, and he asked how many people were coming. I said about one hundred men, and with their wives, about eighty women. A look of concern darkened his face. He said, "David, you're going to have a sausage fest." And I said, "It's okay, you can serve sausage. I'm kosher, but you can serve sausage." And he said, "No, David, this is the Playboy Mansion. We need four or five women for every man. We have a reputation to keep."

I began to sweat. *Where am I going to find 400 women?* Lucky for me, the guy saw I didn't know what I was doing and gave me a hand. He put me in contact with the kind of people who can produce 400 women out of thin air, and everything was ready to go.

Wouldn't you know it, Friday night I got a call from a frantic Paul Stanley. "I lost my voice," he said. "What do I do?" I said, "Paul, just show up. It's more important that you're there jamming with the campers." So he came, and just his presence was enough. It ended up being one of the best camps I ever produced.

DAY 2

ROCK 'N' ROLL BOOT CAMP

The second day of rock camp is when the campers—and the rock stars—realize they haven't signed up for a pleasure cruise. It's going to be a challenge all week. I want to shock the campers. I'll say, "This afternoon you'll be jamming with Steve Morse from Deep Purple, so you'd better be ready. You can't make me look bad or else I won't get these rock stars to come back!" So I put a little fear into them. I also dress up in costumes—I'll go as Gene Simmons or Slash—just to ease the tension. But I want the campers to be on their toes, because it's important that the rock stars enjoy the experience too. Also, I never want to give the campers a layup. I want them to walk out of there having really learned something. I want them to feel like their life has changed. That takes work.

Lita Ford (vocalist): It's not just a few minutes or an hour a week. It's five straight solid days. It's boot camp for rock 'n' roll. By the time it's over, you know everything about their mother and their father. You live with them. It's pretty cool.

Kamesh Nagarajan: For four or five days it's all you're doing. It's like you're imbibing the entire experience. You're standing for fourteen hours, you have roadies who change your strings if they break. You don't really have access to your cell phones. You're really immersed. Your whole life is playing.

Adam Kury: This is a once-in-a-lifetime opportunity. Everyone tries to squeeze every bit of juice out of it as they can. It's that old "I'll sleep when I'm dead" thing.

Amy Edwards (guitarist, vocalist, radio host): Yeah, I didn't sleep very much.

Joe Vitale (multi-instrumentalist, The Eagles, Joe Walsh): It's ten hours of nonstop running around and playing music. You get there early in the morning, you have your third cup of coffee, and you're ready to roll. It's nonstop. There are masterclass rooms, rehearsal rooms, speeches. It's nonstop for about ten hours, because you have a deadline—by the end of the week, you have to play two nights in front of a live audience, and you have to prepare to play a song with the celebrities. You gotta get your band geared up to do that. It's really amazing how quickly campers get into it on day one.

Sammy Hagar: It was the hardest I ever worked in one day in my life.

Spike Edney: Work hard, play hard if you're going to be a rock star.

Sheerin Moss: It definitely is a working vacation. I've been around bands most of my life but never truly realized the hard work involved in getting your chops down.

Greg Deal: In the beginning, you're like, "There's no way this is ever going to happen." Sometimes you have some really green musicians. If you have the right counselor you can overcome that, but it's hard work. Your counselors are working with you day and night. It's a lot of work, but it sure is fun. Welcome to being in a band.

Jack Blades: Day two we all get together in the room with our bands and work out the songs we're going to play and who's going to do what. We have a conversation: "Okay, we have four guitar players. One of you guys has to play bass, who's it gonna be?" Sometimes I'll jump in and play bass if nobody can play bass. Then it's like, "Who's gonna sing it?" Some people bring along a wife or a husband, and the husband's like, "I don't do anything." I say, "You can play cowbell. We're gonna do 'Mississippi Queen,' here's your cowbell. Here's how it goes. Bang-bang-bang-bang-bang. That's your job." He's like, "I run a multimillion dollar hedge fund." Well, now you're a cowbell player.

Angie Mariasine: It's a lot of work. That should be emphasized: it's not all fun and games. The people you're with are fantastic, and you can have a few beers with them, but during the rehearsals, it's tedious work. You're going to perform for the public two days after meeting a band you've never been with before. Everyone has a different skill level. Everyone spent a lot of money to be there, so there's a lot of egos and attitudes. Everyone thinks they're special. And you need to come out with three or four songs that you can nail on stage. All together, you get maybe ten hours of rehearsal before you have to be on stage. And people get scared.

Robert Sarzo: We work so hard. We're striving for the best of the best. It gets a little competitive.

Warren Haynes (guitar, Gov't Mule, the Allman Brothers): It has to be intense. A lot has to be packed into that small window.

Gene Simmons: Rock 'n' Roll Fantasy Camp is not about being ordinary. It's about becoming extraordinary.

Tony Franklin: We start early, and it goes late. It is like being on tour. It's what it's like being in the music business. In some ways, it's more intense, because we're cramming so much into a short amount of time. On tour, you have down time, you have travel time, time in between, but when you're on, you're really in intense focus. At the camp, you're in that intense focus all day. You're always on. Their heads must explode at the end of it. But it's so fulfilling and rewarding.

Britt Lightning (guitarist, Vixen): Things don't happen if you don't work hard.

Michelle Capezza: We did not stop performing and practicing for four days. You're learning all these songs, you're meeting your band, you're meeting the counselors and the headliners. You're a fan and a musician. We did a Viper Room show, we did a Troubadour show. You're at these legendary venues. It was like living the rock-star life.

Joe Vitale: My job is to remind them that, hey man, we're playing with Joe Perry in two days. Let's get this together. They want it. They want to be the greatest. But it takes a lot of work.

David James Smith: You soon stop caring what other people think of you and you just start enjoying it.

Joe Perry: When you're at the camp, all you're thinking about is guitar.

Vinny Appice (drummer, Black Sabbath, Dio): When you come to the camp, you don't think of anything else. You come here and you focus on music. You get to act like a rock star for the weekend. You play music all day, go back to the hotel and go to the bar, hang out. It's like you're in a band on the road.

Simon Kirke: Oh my God, this is hard work. Harder than anything I did with Bad Company or Free. Very few people in my industry are awake and eloquent at nine or nine-thirty in the morning. But it is worth it.

Anthony Mullin: You realize that the rock stars started the same way we did. They were just fans. But then when you play with them, you notice the natural ability and the work ethic. That's when you realize the difference. They try to instill that this is a job. It's not all just the stereotypes of rock 'n' roll. You see how hard they have worked to get to where they are.

Roger Daltrey: It can be extremely hard work. The food is shit, but there again, it was shit when we were young. Rock 'n' roll bands, they eat shit food. It's all part of the fun. Music is a great equalizer.

The harder they work, however, the more the campers and counselors begin to gel. Then comes the moment when it all clicks. The campers start to see the light at the end of the tunnel—they're going to learn what it's really like to be in a band, and get better at their instrument too.

Richie Faulkner (guitarist, Judas Priest): It's such a team environment being in a band. You can learn your instrument at home, but there's so much more to being a musician. You have to listen, work together. And everyone's on the same side. I had to learn that the hard way. This scenario, rock camp, is such a great opportunity for people to work that out. I get chills when I think about it. When you're in a room and something clicks—that feeling, I don't know what it is. I don't think you need to know what it is. You can't quantify it. That's the magic. That's why we're all doing it. That's why everyone is here. That's what we're all looking for. You don't have to say anything. You're in the room with the campers, and you look at them, they look at you, and you don't have to say anything. It's that magic connection.

Spike Edney: In rehearsals, I have my bands set up exactly how they'll be at the big show. I make them take pictures of their amp settings, and have them practice putting their pedals down and making sure the cables are out of the way. Then I make them think about the performance. What are you going to do while you're playing, just stand there like a dumbass? We did staging and choreography. It's about making sure they are fully in the moment, fully aware.

Kelly McPoland: I fell in love with the rehearsal process. It was so cool to see it come together. It's like being in college or high school classes. You start to appreciate other people, and you make good friends.

Brain Tichy (drums, Billy Idol, Whitesnake, Foreigner, Ozzy Osbourne): You couldn't do this in one day. It takes the whole four days. You have to eat lunch, eat dinner with each other, jam all day, go back to the hotel, sleep on it. You have to come together as a band.

Teddy Andreadis: I'm telling you, when you get down into those little cubicles, those concrete cubicles, and you're in there for three or four hours and the A/C isn't working, and you're trying to get a guy who's a shredder to learn a classic rock song, and he doesn't want to do it, you're really in it. But how does David put it? There's no "I" in "band."

Britt Lightning: One camper said, "I wish I could play guitar like you, but I'm just a rocket scientist." I mean, I'm starstruck. Rock camp is a place where you can feel accepted. There's old people, there's young people, there's the head of Oracle and there's someone with a learning disability. We're all equal there.

Sammy Hagar: When you walk out of here, you're going to be a better musician.

*Emmylou Harris posing with a camper
at Songwriting Rock Camp.*

*A camper stands shoulder to shoulder with Johnny A of
The Yardbirds and guitar legend Jeff Beck.*

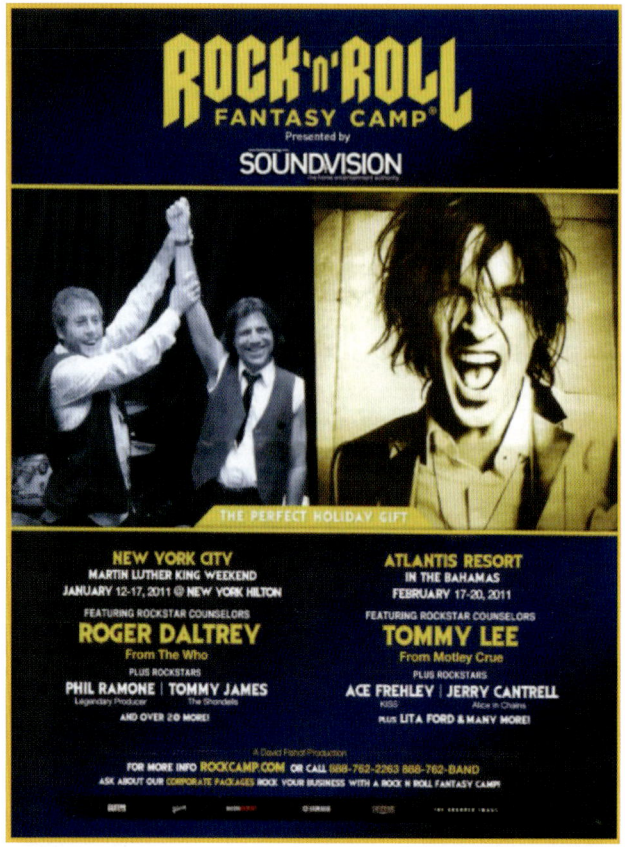

A little help from Sir Roger Daltrey!

Sammy Hagar joins a camper on vocals.

Tag team: camper Miles Schuman gets bass lessons from
Gene Simmons and Bruce Kulick of KISS.

Rudolf Schenker and Matthias Jabs rehearsing
with campers at Scorpions Rock Camp.

Orianthi at the iconic Whisky A Go Go
for the Women Only Rock Camp.

Zakk Wylde performs with a camper onstage in Las Vegas.

Rocking with Sebastian Bach.

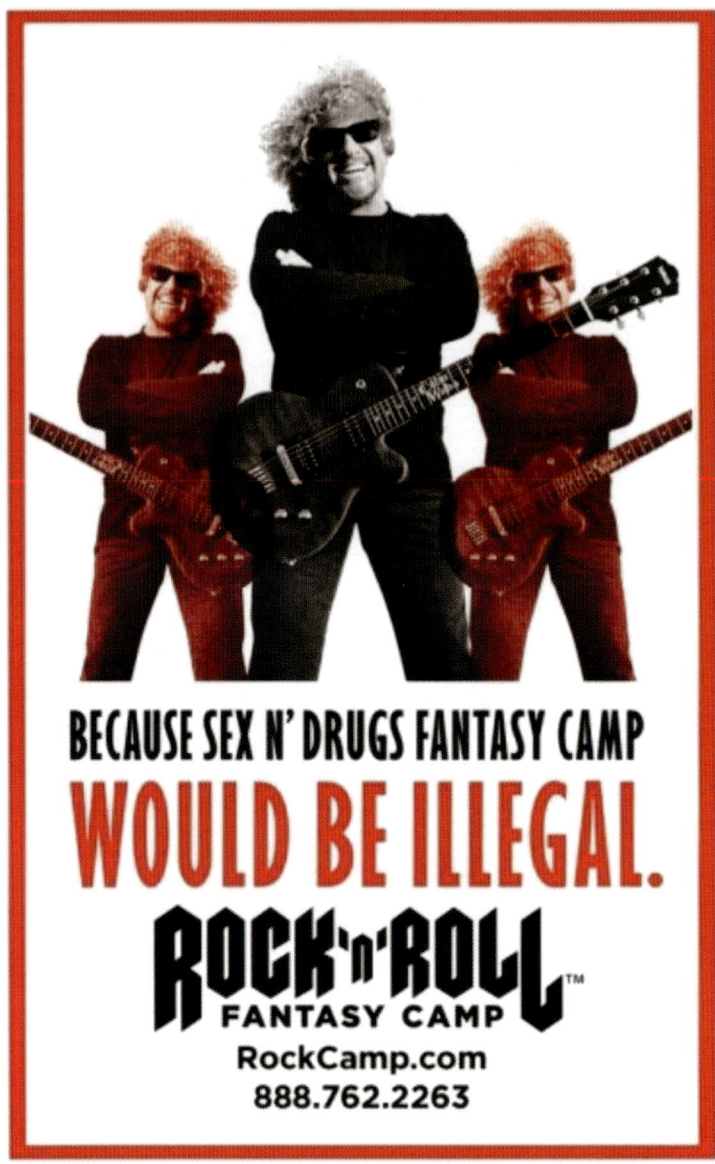

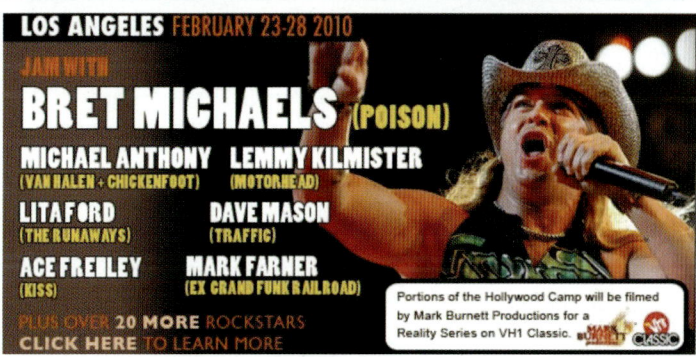

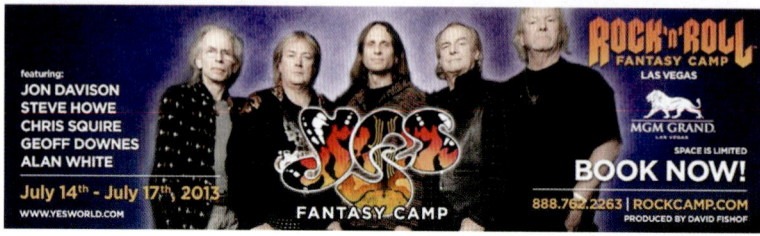

DAY 3

JUMP UP AND DOWN, PASS OUT, CRY

Day three belongs to the special guests. This is the chance for the campers to meet their heroes, not just as fans but as fellow musicians. But that's not all—they also have to get ready for their first big performance. So, in the midst of meeting and playing with the biggest names in the business, the campers are also learning how to perform at the most iconic venues in rock history. It isn't easy to step on stage at the Viper Room, where Tom Petty and the Heartbreakers, Johnny Cash, and Michael Hutchence have performed. It takes guts to give it your all at the Whisky a Go Go, a venue hallowed by the Doors, Led Zeppelin, Van Halen, and too many other legends to name. But rock camp makes the impossible possible. It gives ordinary people the courage, the opportunity, and the impetus to become extraordinary.

Miles Schuman: You spend hours and hours in that rehearsal room playing the same three or four songs over and over again until you have it nailed down. Right when you think you have it nailed down, they bring a rock star in and you realize you don't have it nailed down.

Angie Mariasine: That third day, you realize you're going to have to perform with a rock star on stage, and you feel like you've made a mistake. You're not good enough. You shouldn't be there. And then you get to your first performance. You get up on stage—if it goes bad or if it goes good it doesn't matter—there's a rush. And then there's a euphoric state. Holy fuck, we did it, we pulled it off.

Tommy Mullin: The first day you suck, the second day you're a little better, the third day you're on, man. You're locked in.

Taft Stricklin: My band was working on a song and Phil Collen from Def Leppard walked in: "Hey guys, just want to see how you're doing." I'm thinking, "What just happened?" Then, Sammy Hagar comes in and says, "Hey, whatcha got?" He checked in on the progress throughout the day. When he walked out of the room, I thought, "Between yesterday and today, I can die." How often does the hair on your arms stand up? How many times can you pack that into four days? The nerves that go through your body when you're thinking, "My childhood hero is standing eight feet away from me." I didn't know if I was going to jump up and down, pass out, or tear up and cry.

Rey More: The word "fantasy" is accurate.

Greg Deal: Grand Funk Railroad was a huge band for me, and Mark Farner was an idol. I was scared to death! I came from a small town in Minnesota. We never saw rock stars on TV. For us, we would sit and spin his albums over and over again, and all we had to go on was the pictures in the albums. I told him, "I'd envision myself up there singing with you and drumming with you." That's all we had was the image. When I saw them live, I was beyond excited, and of course it went too fast and it was gone. I never saw him again. And now there I was playing with him. This was something you could only have dreamt about. You dream of just meeting the guy, let alone singing with him. Rock 'n' roll fantasy camp is aptly named. It's a fantasy.

Karen Adams: My fear and excitement were paralyzing when Roger Daltrey walked into our practice space at SIR Studio, but somehow I managed to say hello, gush, and give him a peck on the cheek. He also autographed a photo that I had taken during my first time seeing The Who in concert in Atlanta, in 1980. I pinched myself all day and couldn't stop smiling. The whole camp was like that—a whirlwind of meeting visiting musicians like Dickey Betts, Nils Lofgren, Jon Anderson, and Bret Michaels, sharing meals and stories with other campers, taking photos constantly, and rehearsing our songs.

Nicko McBrain celebrating with campers at Metal Rock Camp.

Ed Oates: Brian Wilson came into our room and said, "Let's go boys!" So we went into "Surfin' Safari." I was doing lead guitar, and he said, "Good tone!" That was cool. He asked if we knew another song. We did "The Thrill Is Gone," and Brian started directing the band on what to play. He still had incredible ears. I had my Carl Wilson Rickenbacker twelve-string. I had him sign the pick guard.

David James Smith: The great glory of the whole experience was I got to sing with Brian Wilson. That guy had been through the mill and back. He looked like he was about 300 years old. But when he opened his mouth and sang, it was still the same old Brian.

Amy Edwards: Tommy Lee came in to hear us one day, and he was so gracious. I think we played a couple of songs. I know one of them was the Cure's "Just Like Heaven," and he was just so nice and he said something encouraging to me that has always stayed with me. He pointed at me and he was like,

"Kip tells me you've only been playing for six months. You're really good, keep it up." I had a heart attack knowing that he and Kip had a conversation about me.

Kip Winger: If you look at the really big rock stars that have come and done it, those are the guys that are the real deal. They're not afraid to roll up their sleeves and hang with the regular people. Those are the real ones. Roger Daltrey. Joe Perry. Guys like that. They're the real deal. Oftentimes the biggest ones are the coolest ones.

Rey More: I'm at a camp, and Rudy Sarzo comes in to lunch. You think of the people he's played with—Ozzy biting the head off a bat. He's the farthest thing from that you can imagine. I found out at this lunch in Las Vegas that Rudy and I have had basically parallel lives. Since then, we've become very close friends. He's one of these guys that, for being a kickass bass player in a metal band, he's one of the gentlest, most thoughtful, most intelligent men that I have ever had the pleasure of meeting. That would only happen at rock camp.

Frank Pawlak: The memories of interacting with rock legends will last forever: exchanging riffs with Warren Haynes on "Midnight Rider," a tune that for me harkens back in a very personal and meaningful way to that other life, when I was a young kid with a guitar and a dream; standing six feet away from Joe Satriani while he played a jaw-dropping solo to "Foxey Lady," after which he shouted, "Frank, take it!" I think all sense of my physical and mental being went black for about five seconds. I remember feeling humbled when Britt Lightning stepped away from her own camp band to personally coach me up on lead guitar.

Angie Mariasine: We all want the autograph, don't get me wrong. But you get to also feel like almost an equal. I actually performed on stage with Buddy Guy. I performed with Ginger Baker. These are the people who made rock what it is. They not only paved the pathway, they created the pathway. And I was able to be on a stage performing with them. People go to the Vatican to touch a statue, to get a glimpse of the Pope. For a rocker, you go to fantasy camp. And not only do you get a glimpse—you get to stand on stage next to them, you get to be in their world. How many people can say that?

Jeff Morris: Most of the time, it's just a meet and greet. You have thirty seconds; they don't even look at you. You're ushered in, you take your picture, and you leave. Or when you're going to see Journey in a 75,000-seat arena, you're just one person. You don't feel like you were connected to the band. But you go to a rock camp, and now you get to sit down with Jonathan Cain and Steve Smith. You get to jam with them. You get to perform with them on a stage. You're going to break bread with these guys. They're going to give you their phone number, and when they come to town, they're gonna get you in. It's such an amazing experience for the campers, the counselors, and the stars.

Jonah Carden (guitarist, ex-data analyst): I got to watch Jerry Cantrell play one of my favorite songs, "Nutshell." He was so close, I couldn't even fit his whole body in the frame of my camera. I had tears in my eyes. When it was finally my time to get up there, Alice in Chains bass player Mike Inez had to go to the bathroom as soon as we got up on stage. I found myself standing right next to Jerry, and we both had a guitar in our hands. I launched into some of his deep cuts, and he started playing with me, impressed that I knew that stuff. Alice in Chains have a lot of harmonies in their songs, and next thing I know, Jerry asked me if I'd sing the harmonies with him. Then he asked me if I knew the solo to the song we were playing. I said, "Yes, but I thought you would do it." He said, "No, I want you to do it." It was a dream come true. That's the great part of the camp. The famous rock stars treat you like an equal, like a friend.

Bruce Hendricks: Playing with Jeff Beck, it's like you're in the huddle with Tom Brady, and he's pointing to you, saying, "I'm going to throw the ball to you."

Joe Perry: It's like the difference between watching football on TV and actually being in the game.

Alice Cooper: To say you played with Kane Roberts and Kip Winger, it's like saying, "I was driving with Mario Andretti. I was acting with Johnny Depp."

Larry Hennessee (guitarist, marketing professional): Anybody who says they weren't starstruck is lying. Even some of the counselors are starstruck.

Dave Basner (MTV executive): Yes, there are huge name stars there, but it's not the normal relationship between fan and rocker—it's more like musician with musician. I'm so used to being in these situations where I'm covering an event and people are going up to these celebrities and saying, "Can I have your picture, can I get an autograph?" Here, it's, "Was that an E or an E flat?"

Don Oates (guitarist, financial planner): The beauty of the camp is that it's more than getting autographs. A minute after Jeff Beck signed my guitar, I was playing it on stage with him.

Rob Halford (vocalist, Judas Priest): There's a purity in it. It's music in its most honest format. When you become a professional musician, you think and behave differently. When you start out, it's full of all of these different mixed-up emotions. In this instance, when you're meeting someone who maybe just learned how to play guitar or play drums, you can sense that. It's such a thrill for us to see that individual go through that exercise and accomplish it, to any degree. We're not bothered about what it sounds like. The fact is you're there and you're doing it. That's the big win. We're in the room doing it together.

Teddy Andreadis: You know, the third day they're jamming on stage playing a Doors song with Robby Krieger on guitar and Todd Rundgren singing. The next day they come in the classroom and go, "I can't believe he was standing right next to me! Where am I ever going to get a chance to do that?"

Rey More: When we played with Roger Daltrey, we didn't have a synthesizer player, so I'm doing the intro of "Baba O'Riley" on guitar. All of a sudden, Roger Daltrey looks me right in the eyes, and I hear, "Out here in the fields," and I almost dropped my guitar on the ground. That was worth the price of admission.

Jeff Morris: When you meet these rock stars, there's that initial moment of, "Oh my God, I worshipped you since I was eight." Then it's like, "Ok, we got work to do."

Even the rock stars get into the spirit of it, often giving more of themselves than I asked.

I remember inviting Nick Mason of Pink Floyd to come for two or three hours; next thing I knew he stayed for four days and jammed with all the bands. Then there was Bill Wyman, who came to our camp in London. Again, I asked him to spend a few hours, but he was having such a good time, he didn't want to leave. It was getting close to sundown, which for me meant it was time to observe the Sabbath—Judaism doesn't have a special exemption for rock 'n' roll. So I said, "Hey Bill, are you ready to go home now?" He said, "No, I'm okay, my family went away for the weekend, I can stay." "But Bill, I have to leave because of the Sabbath." He said, "Well it's not the Sabbath yet in LA!" It touched me to know how badly he wanted to stay. And that is one of my favorite parts of the camp: it's not only the campers who have a life-changing experience. Many of the stars do too.

Tommy Mullin: Some of the musicians that were there, they put their walls down and they start telling things about their writing techniques, their inspirations, things they would never tell anyone. My camp was Stone Temple Pilots and Alice in Chains. It was intriguing because both of them had lost their lead singers to addiction, and they opened up and it got emotional. I mean, when you can ask any question you want and they open up and they're pretty honest, that's incredible. I think they enjoyed it more than they thought they were going to as well.

Amy Edwards: I remember one night we just were all hanging around drinking wine, and we ended up in a room and Mark Hudson just sat there and told us stories that were hilarious. He knew everyone and had stories about Cher, you name it, from back in the day. It was just really cool to get to hear those things that you never would have heard.

Bruce Kulick: Probably the most exciting thing I've ever done musically in my entire life was at the camp in London. Not only did we get to hangout in Abbey Road, I got to jam with Jack Bruce. We played two Cream songs, and I truly became the Eric Clapton for Jack Bruce, and that's one of my heroes. I had a little bit of it recorded on my phone, and I watched it later that night, and I was crying. I mean, the idea of me as a kid dreaming about Cream, and then to actually play those songs and play with my hero was just unbelievable.

Jack Blades: Look, I've played with Ringo, I've written songs with the guys in Journey, I've played with Ted Nugent, but dude, there's nothing like playing on stage at the House of Blues, playing bass on "Won't Get Fooled Again," and here comes Sir Roger Daltrey: "Yyyyyyyeah!" I have goosebumps all over my arms right now just thinking about the experience. It's priceless. But by the end, what I enjoyed most was the connections with the so-called "campers" that have now lasted a lifetime. That's the kind of relationships you build and that's the kind of unexpected positive outcome that you had no idea was going to happen. Not only do their lives change, but my life has changed completely because one of the campers became my best friend. We talk five times a day on the phone. So, it's these unintended consequences that turn out to be the most amazing experiences of your life. The camp creates conditions that could never ever happen any other way. End of story.

Teddy Andreadis: I had a band where the drummer bailed on us. I'm going, "I don't have a fucking drummer, what am I going to do?" No sooner do I say that, Nick Mason of Pink Floyd walks in. He was the special guest that week. I go, "Uh, sir, Nick, would you mind? We don't have a drummer." He says, "I'd love to! I'd love to!" He was our drummer for the whole week. Imagine being in a band and Nick Mason is your fill-in drummer. Where else are you going to get that? Or Gene Simmons would spend a good half hour with each band. If you had thirteen, fourteen bands for that camp, he was there all friggin' day! Or Meat Loaf would come in and we would play a song and he would go, "Okay, you know what? You see, when you sing that part you have to own it!" And he would go, "That guitar part, your bass is a little bit too loud and you don't have enough bottom end to it." He would really just dissect the whole band and after he would leave everybody would be like, "What the hell? That was so cool!" Where else are you going to get Meat Loaf to do that for you?

Scott Hamilton: I was always a gigantic Todd Rundgren fan. He came into my room, and we were playing "Ticket to Ride," but we didn't have a lead guitar. David goes, "Does anybody have any questions for Todd?" I said, "Will you be our lead guitar player at the Whisky a Go Go?" He said, "Sure!"

Greg Deal: I'm drumming next to Tommy Aldridge of Whitesnake, and all of a sudden, my cymbals are crashing. He was reaching all the way across and hitting my cymbals. It scared the shit out of me!

Michelle Capezza: John Oates spent extra time at the camp. He was mingling with everyone. I got to have coffee with him and chat with him. We played "I Can't Go for That" with him. We also did a public performance with him at the Troubadour. We debuted our song, "I'm Sorry," while he watched off stage. So when he walked on stage, he looked at me and said, "That was a great song." I almost died. And then we got to perform together. How do you beat that?

Mark Pontz (bassist, mortgage loan officer): Gene Simmons didn't want to jam with us; he wanted us to write a song and he'd critique it. So we actually ended up writing a cool song. When we played it, he said, "That's a cool riff." Someone told him that I wrote it. Then he wanted to play it with us. He actually ended up playing my bass while it was still strapped on me. KISS was the reason I started playing music, and there I was having a very close and intimate moment with Gene Simmons.

Kelly McPoland: It was an absolute dream come true to sing on stage with Nancy Wilson. After an incredible chance hallway encounter with her the night before our performance, she named our band Purple Heart in honor of her father who served in the military.

Vinny Apice: When I grew up, thirteen, fourteen years old in Brooklyn, we'd say, "Hey, Tony's parents are going to be gone for the weekend. Let's go jam there." We used to jam a lot. That was how we learned. Once you get professional, everything is on a schedule. You're recording, touring, doing interviews, on the road. You don't get to jam or hang loose with musicians anymore. It becomes a business. With the camp, it could be me and Rudy Sarzo, a few campers come in, "Hey, what do you want to play?" And we just start jamming. I tell them, "Man, I haven't done this since I was a teenager."

Rudy Sarzo: In my band was an oil worker, a big burly guy. His son died in a car crash. He came in with a song that he had written. I thought this was something that needed attention, priority, something that could really pull people together in our band. We worked for a couple of days on the song, he had the lyrics, the guys put together some chord changes for him to sing on. A lot of emphasis and time was put into his original song dedicated to his son. Roger Daltrey was going from room to room to meet the campers because he's incredibly cordial, even before he goes into the rooms to do his performances. He came in the room, heard the song, met this gentleman and heard the story, and instead of just walking into the next room, he stayed there, listened to the song, and he was moved to tears. It was an honest emotion. He hugged him. Those are the magic moments.

Kamesh Nagarajan: Before camp started, I called and said, "I'm getting very serious with my girlfriend. Is there a way that Roger Daltrey could help me propose?" They got back to me a few days later and they said, "Listen, we talked to Roger's people and he'd love to help you with that proposal." Less than two days later, The Learning Channel called and said, "We're doing a documentary on the kind of people who go to Rock 'n' Roll Fantasy Camp and we're gonna follow four people's stories for a two-hour documentary. Would you be willing to have us pull you out and talk about your story and obviously have us capture the proposal?" It was all so surreal.

It was awesome, but I'm also thinking I'm going to have to perform. Adding the nervousness of playing on stage with one of your heroes to proposing is that much more, man. The third day, he came into our rehearsal room, and I'm thinking, "Oh, my God, it's Roger Daltrey," but also, my girlfriend was there, and I was afraid he was going to blow the surprise. Sure enough, the first thing he says is, "Hey, who's the bloke who's gonna..." and I tap him, "Ixnay! Ixnay! Roger, I'd like you to meet..." So my first interaction with Roger is telling him to shut up. And then fortunately we did a run through and he was, of course, a pro. He spent a lot of time with me, just like, "Pete Townshend may not play hard chords, but the way he plays it is like no one plays it." After we played, he told me, "Hit it again! Like your hands are gonna fall off!"

And sometimes, the rock stars' lives are changed in ways they could have never imagined. One of my favorite memories is when I finally got Def Leppard to come. Each band was trying to figure out which Def Leppard song they were going to play, and I said, "Listen, I know Joe Elliott is a big Mott the Hoople fan, and if you do "All the Young Dudes," he'll probably love it. So when Joe came in the room, he asked, "What song does this band want to do with me?" I said, "They've got a surprise for you." They started playing "All the Young Dudes," and his eyes lit up. I walked him out to his limo, and he turned to me and said, "David, I just went to Rock 'n' Roll Fantasy Camp."

Another great moment was when Roger Daltrey came to camp. He was going to do a few songs with the counselor all-star band, and he said to me, "I gotta keep singing to keep my voice." So he put Bruce Kulick and the band through a four-hour rehearsal. After it was over,

Bruce came running out and said, "I just went to Rock 'n' Roll Fantasy Camp for four hours with Roger Daltrey!"

Troy Garrity: My counselor was Elliot Easton of the Cars. Somewhere around the afternoon of the first day, he came up to me and said, "I heard you're an investigator. Could I ask you to find someone for me?" I said yes. He told me a story about the one that got away—you know, *the girl.* He said, "There hasn't been a day in twenty-six years that I have not thought about her." That was pretty touching. He was so sincere and intent about how important this was. This was in 2008—we didn't quite have the same technology where it was so easy to find people. He didn't have much to go on, but I said I'd help when I got back home. I got back home and started looking for *the girl.* My first call hit. I found her parents. They were elderly, living on the East Coast. You can imagine, the dialogue in my head was, "Hi, I'm Troy Garrity, I'm a private investigator, I have a rock star client who is looking for your daughter." I didn't know how to say it to this nice old couple. It sounded so bizarre. I'm usually looking for drug dealers or witnesses to homicides. This wasn't really my thing. I told the mother, "If you could contact Jill and let her know that Elliot would love to speak with her, tell her to call me." Within thirty minutes, Jill called me. She said, "I'd love to see Elliot." He was elated. The irony was, she only lived about seventy miles away from him. I forgot about it, several months went by, and I got a wedding invitation from them. The wedding was extraordinary. Elliot played "Here Comes the Sun," and his daughter sang. It was picture perfect.

It's impossible to put the magic of the camp into words, but one sure sign that something special—almost spiritual—is going on is that most people say the big-name stars weren't even their favorite part of camp. Of course, legends like Alice Cooper and Roger Daltrey draw the campers in, but what ends up meaning the most are the relationships the campers form with each other and their counselors, the knowledge they acquire about music and about themselves, the courage they discover that they didn't even know they had, and the realization that it's never too late to live your dreams.

Kip Winger: Most people end up not giving a shit about the big stars. They just want to be there to learn and hang.

Tommy Mullin: Obviously meeting the big-name stars, that's cool. But that was probably maybe the fifth most enjoyable thing of the weekend.

Tony Franklin: They choose counselors very very carefully. We're not only sharing how to play, we're sharing the, shall we say, philosophical, spiritual side of music. Being good at your instrument is really just the starting point. These are skills that help them on a deeper level than just learning how to play a song.

Kane Roberts: In the midst of trying to learn the songs, so many things happen. There's a tremendous amount of activity and dynamics going on that the campers weren't expecting. Maybe they thought they'd just be sitting there waiting for the headliner to come, but it turns into an entirely different experience than they would have thought. Granted, they're excited about the headliners, but we all experience it together. It turns into a rather grandiose communal experience rather than this solo effort.

Larry Harris: It turned out, it wasn't about the idols at all; it was the camp counselors. They're not huge names, but they're well-known people in the industry.

Ed Oates: As you go to more and more of them, you start looking forward more to the campers and the counselors than the headliners. David could say Elvis is raised from the dead and is going to be there, and I'd say, "Oh, great...but is Sandy Gennaro going to be there?"

Vaughan Merlyn (bassist, guitarist, computer software engineer): The most important moments were with the counselors.

Jerry Schwartz: The coolest thing that happened from it was that I made friends with the counselors. I ended up tattooing a couple of them. The first time I walked into the camp, Danny Seraphine of Chicago was in the studio by himself. My knees were knocking together, I was so nervous. He said, "Okay, man, let's kick off the rust." Being with so many good musicians raised my game.

Mark Pontz: The initial thrill for me was that the counselors were such high-level players. Matthew Nelson, Jeff Baxter, Spencer Davis, Simon Kirke from Bad Company. I played a Beatles song with Sandy Gennaro and Kelly Keagy, Jeff Baxter, and a bunch of other great musicians. That's a great memory.

Jeff Scott Soto: I think the campers come away from the experience, they'll always remember more from the counselors than the stars. The stars are only there for a certain amount of time, but we're there for the entire week building friendships, relationships, trust. You can't just get up on stage hoping everyone is going to remember their parts. That trust factor is a huge thing. You realize that someone who is so proficient in their business outside of camp can actually be a ball of nerves, and they're trusting you.

Joe Vitale: For us counselors, we're not just a bunch of crusty old veterans. We're fans too. Even though we may know some of them, to be on a stage with them in this way, to get to play with them, it's fun. I get to play with Joe Perry. The campers are thrilled, but I am thrilled too.

Adam Kury: Counselors get it on all three levels—we get to see the joy of the campers, we get the personal excitement of playing with rock stars, and we get the camaraderie with our fellow counselors.

Kip Winger: It is cool to meet your heroes, and I got to meet a bunch of mine. I got to sing with Roger Daltrey. I became really good friends with Mark Farner. I was a huge fan of Grand Funk. I got to play all the shit I grew up playing. For me it was a fantasy camp too.

INTERLUDE: ROCK CAMP TV

Rock camp has had several incarnations on television, perhaps none bigger than The Simpsons. *When I got the call to do a cartoon rock camp, I immediately said yes. After getting the okay from me, they called Brian Setzer, Tom Petty, Elvis Costello, and a few other rock stars. The next day, an email came to the producers asking if Mick Jagger and Keith Richards could be on the show. The Rolling Stones were about to go on tour, and they wanted a unique way to promote it. Now we were really rolling. The final guest slot was taken by Lenny Kravitz, and the episode, "How I Spent My Strummer Vacation," became a classic and a fan favorite. Mick and Keith have always said it was exciting for them to do it. Tom Petty and Lenny Kravitz said that their families finally thought they were cool after that episode.*

Mike Scully (*The Simpsons* executive producer): We were one episode short, so [writer] Al Jean asked if I would take on an episode. I went through some old story ideas that I had. I always had the first act of a show where Homer winds up on a *Taxicab Confessions*-style show, and he's had a few too many drinks, and he's in the back seat talking about his family and his regrets in life, and that he always wanted to be a rock star, and he says a line I've used many times on my kids: "Marriage is like a coffin, and each kid is another nail." The family is furious with Homer. I always had the first half of the episode up to that point, but I could never figure out what the second half should be.

One day, I was driving to work and listening to the *Howard Stern Show*. He had on as a guest a great guitarist, Leslie West from the band Mountain, and he was promoting this thing called Rock 'n' Roll Fantasy Camp. The idea struck me in the car—instead of the family being furious with Homer, what if they thought he actually had a point? He did sacrifice his dreams to be a dad, a provider who goes to his job every day that he hates. Once I had that flip of attitude, where they thought he was kind of making sense, and then they thought what can we do for him to thank him for all the sacrifices he made? Well, they send him to Rock 'n' Roll Fantasy Camp.

Once we had that, the rest of the episode just clicked into place. Then it was a matter of figuring out who should be our camp instructors. As fate would have it, one of the heads of Gracie Films got a call from the Rolling Stones' manager. They were getting ready to do a tour the next year and asked if there was anything they could do on the show to promote the tour. She knew I was working on this episode and said, "What would you think if Mick and Keith were on the show?" And, of course, Tom Petty had been up all night recording in the studio and came straight to us at like ten in the morning. And he had been rubbing it in to the Heartbreakers that he had to come be on *The Simpsons*.

It was received really well. *Entertainment Weekly* listed it as one of the top twenty-five episodes we ever did.

We also did a two-hour television special on TLC. The idea started as a full series, sort of The Bachelor *meets rock camp. They wanted to put a young girl jamming with an older guy at camp, hoping that sparks would fly. Luckily Roger Daltrey talked me out of it. He said, "You have such a great brand, don't ruin it like that. Go back and tell them that you'll do a documentary and I'll do it for you. And that's how the two-hour special came on TLC, (it's currently on YouTube).*

Soon after, Citibank did a Rock 'n' Roll Fantasy Camp commercial that ran for fourteen months. Now business began to pick up. Still, I wanted my own series. It remained a dream until I got a call from Mark Burnett's office. He said, "I want to make a reality show." At that time I had ten offers from ten different producers, but Mark was the biggest guy in town. He sold the show in twenty-four hours to VH1 Classic, and Lee Metzger produced it.

Lee Metzger (producer, *The Apprentice, The Voice*): I was working on a television show and heard about the camp. I'm a musician. I used to be in a hair band in L.A. I thought I'd go check out the camp as a camper. We didn't tell anyone I'd be producing the show. I wanted to see how it worked. I did four days, and I realized we needed to make some changes to make it a TV show because the camp is just about jamming all day, which is great, but it doesn't make a television show.

We made the show for VH1 Classic. The first season, our counselors were Mark Hudson, Kip Winger, and Rudy Sarzo. I can't say enough nice things about them. Rudy is unbelievably gracious. The idea of the show was to do a five-episode doc series. We'd have people audition, and the camp counselors would choose the anchors for the bands—drummer, singer, guitarist, and so on. Each counselor put together a band of five. We got them rehearsal space at CenterStaging, which is where the Stones rehearse. We had the rooms designed by a production team. It really upped the ante. We made them hit the ground running. Pick a name for the band and go.

Learn a song and go play it at the Whisky. After that, each day was a new event. There was a gig every night. They were playing big venues. We were putting them through their paces. Over the course of the two seasons, we brought in really great rock names: Paul Stanley, Sammy Hagar, Bret Michaels, Ace Frehley. For the end of season one we put together a supergroup to jam with these guys. It was really cool.

DAY 4

YOU'VE NEVER SEEN SMILES THIS BIG

The whole camp builds to the final day of performances. We book some of the most famous rooms in rock history, from the Whisky a Go Go in L.A. to the Cavern Club in Liverpool, and give the campers a chance to get on stage and show what can be done when you throw a handful of strangers into a room for a week with a rock star and make them learn to play together. This is not just a victory lap or a chance to show the spouse and kids what mommy or daddy learned at camp. This is a concert featuring some of the biggest names in music, and it attracts quite an audience. Everyone from Joaquin Phoenix, to Steve Perry, to Prince has been spotted in the crowd, watching the bands on the final night. Prince was doing American Idol *the next night, and he wanted to see what it was like to perform with amateur musicians.*

Dave Basner: When they play that final show, you are witnessing something these people will never forget for the rest of their lives. You've never seen smiles this big. You wouldn't imagine that the human face could support these smiles.

Tommy Mullin: You're doing thirty or forty songs a day for four days, and by that last day, you just pray that you can get on stage and hit those notes. You don't want to embarrass yourself amongst your peers. It's not competitive, but competitive juices flow and you don't wanna suck. We performed on Saturday night at the Lucky Strike in L.A. Saturday night we went on first out of all thirteen bands, and then on Sunday night we went dead last, and let me tell you, going on first is a lot easier than sitting and waiting for three hours.

Joe Vitale: By the fourth or fifth day, man, they are rock 'n' roll stars.

Meat Loaf: To go on stage, you have to have an ego. But ego and ego trip are two different things.

Greg Deal: The last day is a different set of nerves. The rest of the week, you're in a private room. It's just you and your band. But then you're going, "OK, we're going to the Whisky tonight. It's going to be packed. Now we're performing for a crowd."

Adam Kury: The last day is part performance, part party. The work's done. They've put in the rehearsal. Now they get to lay it out and live the dream.

Kamesh Nagarajan: By the final show, you build a brotherhood. You're a band. You're not just trying to get the song; you're trying to help the other person shine as well.

Karen Adams: I remember standing on the stairs listening to the band before us. The music was so loud it was forcing my heart to beat in rhythm with it. It blocked everything out of my mind, including the words to the song we were about to perform. I grabbed our drummer Kevin's sleeve and screamed in his ear, "I've forgotten all of the words!" He knew exactly what to say. He told me to take some deep breaths, and that when our band started the opening notes of the song, the words would come to me. They did, thank God, but boy, my knees were shaking, and I had a serious case of cottonmouth. Then Roger Daltrey came out on stage with us for "[I] Can't Explain." We played the song just as it was in The Who's studio version released in 1964—two minutes and five seconds of magic.

Camper Karen Adams made this lovely drawing of her band and Roger Daltrey on the final night at the House of Blues.

Rey More: We got to the Whisky a Go Go, and I remember going to the barmaid on the second floor, and I said, "I bet Jim Morrison threw up in that corner." She said, "Yeah, and I bet they haven't cleaned it up yet." This is the place where rock history happened. When it's over, you keep replaying it back in your mind. It starts acquiring mythical properties.

Miles Schuman: At the final performance at the Whisky a Go Go, all the rock stars came out and played with the bands. There's nothing cooler. It doesn't really get better than that. I was at the most legendary venue in L.A., waiting for the bathroom, and Rob Halford walked out. His hands were still wet. He flicked the water on me and said, "You've been blessed by the metal god." Then all the rock stars are backstage reminiscing. You're at a place that is a part of music history, with people who are part of music history, looking at what millions of people would die to see—you know, the right side of Rob Halford's face.

Sheerin Moss: Before the final performance, I was changing in the bathroom backstage only to hear a knock on the door. It was Rob Halford: "Is anyone in there? I need to take a leak." That was surreal. And the performance was amazing. I did it. I sang on stage with Rob Halford, *the metal god.*

Lee Mackson: Having never played in a band before, I'm now playing at the Viper Room and the Whisky a Go Go. The rock stars could not have been nicer, particularly Ian Paice of Deep Purple, who has been drumming for sixty years. I was watching him play before us, and he dropped a stick. He said, "Everyone was a beginner at some time. I just dropped a stick!" This guy who is in the Rock and Roll Hall of Fame, and he couldn't have been nicer.

Bruce Hendricks: The day of the performance, I just had this big shit-eating grin on my face. *I'm on stage with Jeff Beck!* It's not something you think could possibly ever happen in your lifetime. I was surprisingly calm. We started playing, and I'm playing the best I've ever played in my life. I don't know if it was because I rose to the occasion or Jeff inspired me, but it was great. We were playing Jimi Hendrix's "Fire," and I'm standing two feet from Jeff Beck watching him play. I'm thinking, "This is the greatest fucking thing since my daughter was born." I don't even know how to compartmentalize it. Then the most remarkable thing in the most remarkable day happened. We're building to the lead guitar solo in "Fire," and I'm watching Jeff, and he looks confused, like he doesn't remember how the solo goes. There's an audience there, and I know they came to see Jeff Beck rip; they didn't come to see Bruce Hendricks rip. But I had to make a decision. Finally, I decided, I gotta take the solo. I don't think Jeff knows it. I made that fateful decision, and I ripped it. I can still see the look on Jeff's face. The song ended and I was electrified. I absolutely nailed the solo. But I didn't know if I read the situation right. As I was coming off stage, Mark Farner of Grand Funk Railroad was in the front row. He said, "I know what you did." Before I could respond, he added, "You did the right thing."

Frank Pawlak: Nothing was greater than "teaching" Cheap Trick's Rick Nielsen how to play the closing to his own band's version of "Lucy in the Sky with Diamonds." I was coming up the stairwell to the backstage second floor of the Whisky, and I heard Rick say, "I'm doing 'Lucy in the Sky,' but I don't know how to end the song." I said, "Rick, I'm in the band doing the tune with you." Rick said, "Come on and show me how the song ends." We went to the practice room down the hall, where my lead singer Scott happened to be sitting. I pulled out my guitar and taught rock legend Rick Nielsen how to play the end of a song he had recorded. Scott asked, "What the hell just happened? I thought you were bringing Rick in to get your guitar signed. Did you just teach him how to play 'Lucy in the Sky?'" I said, "I think so." We fist-bumped and yelled at each other.

Jerry Schwartz: Our big show was at the House of Blues. We played with Steve Vai at noon. While we were on stage with him, over on the side of the room, Joe Perry was standing in the doorway watching us play the song with Steve Vai. Can you imagine Joe Perry in the audience watching you on stage with Steve Vai? And then Steve Vai asked me to do a solo, and my head almost exploded. Then we played "Toys in the Attic" with Joe Perry a few hours later. That night, we played with Eric Johnson on stage and Michael Anthony from Van Halen. When you're on stage with Michael Anthony, and you hear that background Van Halen vocal, it's like hearing him on the records. It's beyond words to explain what that feels like. That was the best day of my life.

Kamesh Nagarajan: You're out there, and there's Roger Daltrey, and he's looking at the guitarist, because he's used to looking at Pete Townshend, except instead of Townshend, it's you! And you think, "I just got a nod of approval from Roger friggin' Daltrey!"

Ed Oates: There's usually some rough stuff going on in the rehearsal rooms, but once it gets on stage, everyone pulls it off. Occasionally there's a train wreck, but very rarely. I attribute that to the people who are there and want to do good, but also to the counselors, who are able to pick songs that meet the level of their band.

Kane Roberts: One of my campers was a beginner. I said, "I'm going to give you a few notes to play for a solo." He said, "I can't do a solo." I said, play these three notes; you have to go home with something. He ended up jumping out in front of everyone on stage and doing all the moves. He's playing three notes like he's Eddie Van Halen. Maybe the solo wasn't so great, but he went home with something special.

Peter Gatti: When I got on the stage and we started playing, I remembered why I once did this. There is no greater feeling in the world, period.

Angie Mariasine: The rock stars get up there with nonprofessionals like us, and they still perform like they're performing for 100,000 people. That's why we come back.

Karen Adams: I was reborn on that stage that night. It opened me up to see who I really am. I learned that I had the courage to be me. It was one of the top five events of my life.

Kamesh Nagarajan: After the show, I invited my girlfriend on stage. I'm wearing leather pants, a foo-foo rock outfit onstage. She's got this leather outfit on. And Roger goes to the mic and says, "Kamesh has been a great Who fan over the years. He's supported this band in good times and bad, and we're really honored to have him as a friend." I don't know where that came from, but I might marry Roger right now. Then he handed me an "award," which was really my proposal, which I had written out, and he said, "I think you should read this." I gave it to my girlfriend to read, and at this point, everyone kind of pulled away. It's just me and her and Roger. But I'm looking out in the crowd and there's four hundred people, and they realize what's happening. In that moment, my girlfriend realizes it's a proposal and goes *gasp!* and she keeps her composure to kind of read through it. Now, I'm wearing leather pants. Not a norm for me. I've got the ring and the box in my pocket and you know, the pants have kind of shrunk. I couldn't get the ring box out of my pocket! And Roger said, "Hey mate, I'm not helping you with that." So I'm struggling to get it out. I finally got it out. "Will you marry me?" I'm on my knee. She turns and looks at me and says, "Yes." The place goes crazy. Roger walks to the mic. He's like, "Kamesh, what would you have said if she said no?" And I said, "Roger, I would've joined the band, right?"

INTERLUDE: BEST BAND NAMES

One of the most fun parts of camp is watching the campers name their bands. Here are some of my favorites:

- Ask Dr. Stupid
- Age Against The Machine
- The Millionaire Playboys
- Led Hefner
- The Cherry Poppin' Virgins
- One Hot Chick
- The Beef Puppets
- Prenuptial Ejaculation

- Viagra Falls
- Fall Out Boob
- Dammit Dammit Dammit
- The Black Shabbos
- Cheap & Nasty
- Fuster Cluck
- Lawyers Drugs and Money
- Irrehearsable
- Steroids To Heaven
- Cap'n Crunch & the Cereal Killers
- Chip Z'Nuff-Drugland Weekend
- Apprentice Dominatrix (named after a camper who was a dominatrix)
- Interstellar Highway
- Smack Daniels
- Collective Bad
- Bleeding Rainbow
- Too Many Cooks
- Purple Strangers
- Vlad and the Impalers
- Mythral Hobbit Ears
- Voodoo Mood
- Hookers and Eight Balls
- Whole Lotta Balls

INTERLUDE: EXTRA! EXTRA! ROCK CAMP IN THE PRESS

Every time someone from the press asked to come watch the camp, I said no. Watching it isn't good enough. You must immerse yourself in the experience. Over the years, we've had great press, and I believe the reason is that we don't just let them see the camp; we make them feel it. We've had some big names come through. I'll never forget when Rob Sheffield of Rolling Stone *came. My dream was to have a story in* Rolling Stone, *but for reasons I still don't understand, Rob's story never came out. Then, in 2014 Rob wrote his book* Turn Around Bright Eyes, *and he dedicated a whole chapter on going to the camp. It made a big enough impression on him that, even though* Rolling Stone *wouldn't publish it, he needed to tell the story.*

Then there was the time Conan O'Brien came to camp. I approached him as he watched the bands rehearse, and I said, "Conan, will you mention us in your monologue?" His answer: "No, David, I'm not going to make fun of you because this is really serious. I'm a guitar player and I really appreciate what these people are going through." We had a similar experience with Maxim *magazine. They sent a writer, but just like with* Rolling Stone, *the article never appeared. I called the writer and he said, "David, I'm not going to submit the story. They wanted me to make fun of your camp. And I'm not going to make fun of your camp."*

I think that speaks to the power of Rock Camp. No matter your preconceived notions, once you see it in action, you can't help but be carried away. Perhaps the greatest example of this was with Liam Gowing of the Los Angeles Times. *I'll let him tell it.*

Liam Gowing: I come from a musical family. I started a band in seventh grade, had a band in college, did some club shows in Los Angeles. I goofed around on drums, but I wasn't a drummer by any stretch. I fell out of music and then started writing about music, and finally got a staff job at the *Los Angeles Times* doing a preview/review column called "Action Man," in which I would do things that the general public could do and give my first-hand experience of it. One of the things I did was the fantasy camp. When I sent in my paperwork, I said, "I'll do whatever you want. Guitar, bass, sing, and drums." I was very cavalier about the drums, and of course David put me on drums. I was so nervous. They called my bluff! They said, "Don't worry, we've got you in the band with another drummer." Which was even worse. Two drummers who aren't great.

Mark Slaughter was our camp counselor. We had a really interesting mix of people. We had a fourteen-year-old guitar whiz kid, a twenty-one-year old beautiful blonde blue-eyed girl, a sixty-something-year-old bass player, a couple of fortyish lawyers on guitar, and Chris Gailfoil, who was the other drummer. I knew nothing about him when I walked in the room, but his mother and sister were there and they told me his story. He had been battling stage four colorectal cancer for over a year and a half. For him to have had it that long and still be at the camp was a testament to his character, but he was in dire straits. His mother said, "He won't make it to Christmas," and this was November. He'd been to a camp in New York, and David was so taken with him, he said, "If you make it to the next camp, it's on me." I think part of the reason he was alive is because David gave him this gift.

I was well aware of the fact that this was probably his last go on Earth. I was terrified, thinking if I play great, which wasn't likely, and show him up he's going to have a bad time, and if I'm a wreck and I fuck him up, then I'm goin to ruin his last experience on Earth. I talked to him and got to know him. At first, we had nothing in common. He was more into metal, prog rock. I was more into classic rock, alternative, grunge. It was really difficult, to say the least. To see him there, taking morphine for the pain, it was pretty rough. There were times over the five days when he'd be sitting at the drums, slipping into unconsciousness. He struggled to keep his strength up.

That camp was amazing. Roger Daltrey was there, Slash, Joe Walsh, Vince Neil. It was mind-boggling to see all those legendary musicians. We'd be in a situation where Chris would have his eyes closed and one of the big stars would come in the room. We'd have to shake him and tell him, "Hey, Roger Daltrey is here," and he'd snap back into it. His love of music and playing drums carried him through it. This guy who should have been in a hospital bed—the rock camp kept him alive. The Grim Reaper was at the door, and he was like, "Not today. I've got to go to Rock 'n' Roll Fantasy Camp."

Liam Gowing (left) and Chris Gailfoil

For our last performance, I didn't have a pair of drumsticks. I borrowed my sticks from Chris. We played at the House of Blues in Vegas, and I spoke to him afterwards and we thanked each other. I knew it was the last time I would see him. I said, "Here are your drumsticks." He said, "Those are yours now. You earned them."

He died sixteen days after the camp ended.

I went home to write. My column was a tongue-in-cheek column to begin with, and I was looking for some angle, thinking it was going to be just a funny thing, but the day after I got home, I broke down in tears. I was bawling because of Chris. It was tears of sadness and joy. I knew Chris went out swinging.

5

HANGOVER: THE RELIGION OF ROCK

I always warn the campers on the last night that my goal is to take them to such a high that they'll be sad when it's over. It doesn't matter whether you're a rock star, a CEO, or a housewife, when the camp ends, it's hard to go back to normal life. Many campers experience a sort of hangover from the excitement. When the dust settles, they often find they've been changed in profound ways. And they can't wait to come back. They get addicted. I don't get a hangover, of course, because I have to start working on my next camp. For me, it is a challenge to keep coming up with more ideas and more stars and more concepts. But to see the reward, to have people contact me every day and tell me how the camp changed their life, that's my addiction.

Angie Mariasine: I've been to eleven camps. People always ask me, Why do you go back? It's the community. Everybody wants to know, Where do I belong? Some people find it in religion. This is the religion of rock.

Greg Deal: When it's over, it's like letting the air out of a balloon. You have a couple days where you're spent. You have to recover. But it's a nice feeling.

Lee Mackson: Work sucks for at least a week after the camp. Returning to normal life is just horrendous. It's called rock fantasy camp for a reason—it's a fantasy. You're on a tremendous high. Even now just talking about it, it refreshes the feeling of how amazing a time it was.

Rey More: After the camp, you're on a high. I take an extra day, I hang around and decompress. I'm retired, so I don't have to go back to work. You can't think of anything else. I call it the "campover." It's like a hangover, but it's because the camp is over. My wife basically calls time out after a couple of days when all I've been doing is talking about camp.

Bruce Kulick: You get through it on that adrenaline of how much the campers are just so excited to be there, but by the end, you're completely exhausted.

Jeff Morris: When you're on the plane ride home, you'll be thinking, "I can't believe this just happened."

Taft Stricklin: When it's finished and you're going home, you hop out of the van at the airport and you're just walking on clouds. It's cleansing for your soul. Here you are with these people, you're creating musically, and you just open your whole soul to everybody. You gotta open it up, or there's no reason to pay the money to go. You're either in or you're out, and if you're in, you gotta go in full tilt. For anyone who is experiencing any kind of burnout—work burnout, political burnout, family burnout—it's a life-changing experience. Almost a decade later, I'm still in touch with these people I connected with on such a deep level. The fact that in four days, you can build a bond with humans that stays and sticks, this is better than any drug. It's better than any quick-fix pill. The pressure of having to perform, having to work together—this is a team, you don't know me, I don't know you, I don't know your ability, you don't know my ability, I don't know your story, you don't know my story. But when you start making music, you understand each other. Going to rock camp makes you realize how magical it is to collaborate.

Ed Oates: There's definitely a post-camp letdown. You're going home and you think, "Those guys I was playing with, I'm not going to see them again maybe until the next camp." Then you think, "Well, what's the next camp, David?" I've been to about twenty camps now. You also keep up the relationships between camps. I've seen Brian Wilson three or four times at shows and he recognizes me when I go backstage. When Gary Hoey comes through town, we get dinner. You get a connection you're unlikely to make any other way.

Jeff Morris: That first camp is like the first hit. You have to keep coming back for more. I've been to close to fifteen camps now.

Bruce Hendricks: I've worked with some of the biggest movie stars and greatest directors of all time. I've had incredible moments on movie sets. I got to meet Paul Newman and Sean Connery. But I've never had a moment like I did at rock camp.

Teddy Andreadis: The last day is the hardest because you have to say goodbye to these people who you've now met and who've become your friends. I still speak to them all the time.

Tommy Mullin: Everything that I expected, it wasn't. Everything that I didn't expect, it was. I was expecting a high-paid meet and greet. And it really wasn't. The camaraderie with the other campers, the musicians, it was just like a soul fraternity.

Robert Sarzo: It becomes a family. We eat together. We talk about life. Every break, we're together. That's what I've always enjoyed about being in a band—getting in a tour bus and talking about life. For those four days, we really gel. It becomes a bond. When they go back home, they don't want to lose that bond. When I'm on tour, the campers come and visit me. I give them backstage passes. They become friends.

Vaughan Merlyn: I can't imagine anybody going through that camp and it not being a life-changing experience. It's almost too good to be true.

Amy Edwards: I remember getting back from it and being on a high, feeling like I could take on whatever I wanted to do musically and having a newfound sense of drive and determination and excitement about it.

Michelle Capezza: Everything you dream of, we did. I just can't wait to do it again.

Lee Metzger: Very few people in the real world have the opportunity to stop worrying about what they *have* to do and focus on what they *want* to do. The camp gives the opportunity, for a few days at least, to stop worrying about paying the bills, and getting the kids to soccer practice. You can check out from the real world. It's a fantasy island. You're staying in a hotel every night. And then when you put people in a band, there's a great camaraderie. And this is a heightened version of being in a band, so the camaraderie is instantaneous. How can you beat that?

Brian Tichy: I sometimes take it for granted, but then I remember that before the camp, this sort of thing just couldn't happen. You could never meet and jam with your idols. There was just no way. Even if you were some really rich guy and you could hire your favorite band to perform for you, it wouldn't be the same. Because you're spending all day with these people you idolize, people who have spent their lives making music. You're getting to eat with them and talk to them, see what it's like to just spend time together making music. You can't get this experience anywhere else.

Tony Franklin: I have ended up making some lifelong friendships with both campers and fellow counselors, and sharing some very significant, life-changing moments. It's amazing to watch how the camp changes people. Beyond just having an experience of four days of interactions with their heroes, the campers are inspired, they feel like they can accomplish things they didn't think were possible. There is a deeper value. It's more than an amusement park ride. It's hard to describe, but it's also hard to describe what it's like to write a song. It is enriching and nurturing something that's pretty deep. You wouldn't think you'd get that from a fantasy camp.

Britt Lightning: Everybody's just glowing on the last day of camp. Any amount of work is worth that. People end up coming back just to get that glow again. After a while, they don't even care who the headliner is. It's like a family reunion. It's a love fest.

Joe Vitale: I don't know of anybody who went home disappointed. They take home encouragement, which is a very important word, and inspiration, another big word. They also have a feeling of self worth. They find out that they're good enough, it just takes a little bit of work.

Jeff Scott Soto: It truly is like a camp when you're a kid. You build new relationships and friendships, in such a short and intense period of time, and then it ends. And it's heartbreaking. The good thing is you know it's not the end. There will be other camps.

Larry Hennessee: Once you go, you're part of this rock 'n' roll club that is fairly exclusive, that gets to jam with rock stars, and share that excitement for the rest of your life. It isn't just four days; it's the first four days of the rest of your life. From that point forward, something's changed in you.

Kip Winger: The thing about rock camp, the way David has it set up, it's the perfect place to go in and be enlightened. Everyone leaves with a bit of spiritual enlightenment. It feels great to give people something that's meaningful and that they can take away with them and get themselves further down whatever path they want to be on. If I can help with that, that's the greatest part. It feels great when you see the light bulb go off on someone's head, and they get it. It's really special. I just got goosebumps.

Simon Kirke: I've seen people in tears on the last day. Grown men in tears.

Kane Roberts: When that week had ended, in my mind, I felt that the "rock stars" got as much out of the experience as the campers. It's about communicating and relating to other people. It's a direct injection, an extreme dose of that in about four days. You learn about their lives, the emotions from their successes and failures, you have to help them, you see the different personalities and you have to help them form into a band. It's such a human experience.

Rey More: Joe Vitale became a friend from the camp. He's one of the nicest people in rock 'n' roll. He called me and said, "I'm touring with Joe Walsh and I'd like to see you." I'm at the arena about forty-five minutes before start time and I get a text from Joe asking if I got my backstage passes. He would not stop until he got them in my hands. It's mind-boggling that this guy goes through that amount of trouble for me.

Kip Winger: I've met some of my best friends in camp, people who will be lifelong friends.

Spike Edney: If they don't go home absolutely fucking exhausted, with their mind in a whirl, then I haven't done a good job. They need to wake up when it's done and say, "What the fuck was that all about?" I wouldn't do it more than once every couple of years because it's so bloody exhausting.

Tommy Mullin: Flying home on the plane, I was exhausted. I said, Jesus, professional musicians and artists earn every penny. You have to have an absolute passion for it because it's exhausting.

Jack Blades: When camp is over, I sleep for five days straight. Because I didn't sleep for five days before. There is no rest for the wicked, brother.

Lita Ford: You can't explain it unless you do it.

6

LESSONS

The camp is about more than just meeting rock stars. It's about learning how to listen, how to cooperate, how to work together to form a whole that is bigger than the sum of its parts. Most people wouldn't associate profound life lessons with rock music—the genre of sex, drugs, and trashed hotel rooms—but that's exactly what the camp does. It leaves everyone better, not just as musicians, but also as people.

Jeff Morris: A lot of people at the camp are used to being in charge. They come into camp and say, "I know what I'm doing." And then all of a sudden, Bruce Kulick is saying, "That isn't right." Now you're taking direction. It's a job, and your job is to be sharp on your parts, so when you perform with these people, you're not embarrassing yourself or anyone in your band. That's the growth—step out of the comfort zone.

Bruce Kulick: I'd get these CEOs—these are the people that no one tells them what to do, because they're the boss. I'm not being rude to them, but I'm basically telling them what to do. Most of the time, it works out. All those people in power, they respect it, because they know that I know what I'm doing.

Bjorn Englen (bassist, Soul Sign, Dio Disciples): You've got people who are bosses, CEOs of companies, and they're not used to someone telling them what to do. There's one or two in each band. That becomes a bit of a challenge. The counselors have to figure out how to deal with all these personalities. It's fascinating. Most of the time, it helps them learn to take direction rather than give it. They'll go back to the hotel, come back the next day, and you know they've been practicing all night. It's really cool.

Larry Hennessee: I've watched it change people's lives.

Jeff Scott Soto: I didn't realize I naturally had that knack of wanting to teach and share. It taught me something new about myself as an artist.

Karen Adams: Rock Camp opened me up to see who I really am. I grew up in the Baptist church as a kid, spent my life trying to be a recovering fundamentalist. The camp had this feeling of, "Oh my God, I've been saved. I've found the real me." I was pushed out of my comfort zone. I chose to do this knowing I would get pushed a little bit, but I had no idea how far I was going to get pushed out of my comfort zone. I remember standing backstage before the big performance thinking, "What the fuck have I done here? I have lost my mind." It was putting myself in situations I had never been in before. It was life before the camp and life after the camp for me. It was a catalyst. It was the best vehicle for me to become me. It was like an explosion. I remember coming home and feeling so changed. I had sort of lost my identity. I think that's why I loved The Who. So much of their music was about identity. "Who Are You?" I loved that music. It felt like my personal anthem. It jolted me awake.

Jerry Schwartz: The whole experience was a life-changing thing. My inspiration growing up was musicians. It wasn't my parents like it's supposed to be. Those were the people I was trying to get away from. To me, my role models were Aerosmith, heavy metal guys. That was how I survived. Music was an outlet that brought me happiness. Growing up, there was a huge mystique to bands, to buying the albums and going to the concerts. These guys were like gods. I overdosed a couple times in my life. In 1993, I was doing crack, cocaine, drinking. I was inspired to get off drugs by Aerosmith. I thought, wow, if Aerosmith can do it, maybe there's hope for me. I was down and out at that time in my life. If you told me when I was thirteen, "Someday you'll be playing on stage with Joe Perry," I'd say, "What are you smoking?" But the rock camp made it happen. And Joe Perry was great. I talked to him for a while before we got on stage. I said, "Thanks for inspiring me."

Tommy Mullin: It does change your life, regardless of whether you want it to or not. The feeling of accomplishment when you're done, and the goodwill you've established with these people you've never known, from all over the world, it's really phenomenal. I left the camp with a feeling that, you know what? I'm in my mid fifties, I need to do more in life. During this pandemic, I started writing music again, which is something

I should have been doing for the last fifteen years, but I've been busy with my career. I alway said I want to write songs for movie scores, for short films and this and that and I still do. It's not too late, and the camp gave me the kick in the ass I needed.

Jack Blades: I've seen it over and over and over with the camp: people tell me how it changed their lives. Music is the common thread in all of us. That's the takeaway. It unlocks everything inside of you. It opens you up, it makes you vulnerable. It makes you cry, it makes you laugh. It makes you want to sing all the time, it makes you want to jump for joy, it makes you want to tap your feet. It makes you want to not sleep, you just want to think about music again.

Joe Perry: I was worried it would be just a big fan thing, a meet-and-greet, and that's a part of it, but anyone who does it is pretty serious about their playing. I see myself on the other side. It's really inspiring. In doing that, I've revisited some of my old things, and very often the people at the camp have a few things that I can learn from them.

Warren Haynes: The cool thing about the camp is someone like me can learn from someone who just started playing, because it's an endless well. It's an ocean of music that we can all learn from.

Max Weinberg: It's quite a fascinating atmosphere of togetherness. They really build bonds. It's very much a giving thing.

Joe Vitale: I had somebody's wife contact me and thank me profusely because ever since her husband came back from camp, he's got his old instrument out and is back into it. He was kind of depressed and the camp just kicked him in the butt and inspired him so much, he got back into it, he's playing music, putting a band together. When the campers go home, they have a new musical life.

Frank Pawlak: It made me a more experienced musician. It also sharpened my intuitive skills and made me a better manager of my team of professionals back home. And it goes without saying that my self-confidence soared to the stratosphere. If I could step on stage at the Whisky a Go Go and play music, I could do anything that my profession commanded. But those memories are secondary to what I think the camp is all about: the power of unifying people through music in a radiant and powerful way.

Mark Farner: What I take home is the love and the stories the campers tell me about who they were with when they heard a song that changed their life, or that they stayed off drugs because of Grand Funk Railroad. You hear these stories, and then you're in there jamming with them, and you have a family that's getting closer together, all based on love. That's my reward. Love is a rewarder of those who diligently seek it.

Warren Haynes: I loved that everybody was passionate about the music. The fans became the musicians and the musicians became the fans. We reminded ourselves why we started playing in the first place. Musicians are the biggest fans. That's how we started out. That's what made us want to go further, to learn how to sing or learn how to play an instrument. It's nice when you're reminded why you started and you see the same passion in someone else.

Sammy Hagar: When they leave camp, they've done something like climbing Mount Everest. It's one big check off the bucket list. I think people get more out of this than any of us know. But I get something too. I see these people getting off—a plumber, a doctor, a lawyer. They would love to play music for thirty hours in a row. They can't get enough. And here I am, this jaded rock star, been doing it my whole life, consider it my job, and I'm going, I don't want to work that hard. Because of Fantasy Camp, a light came on to me about how lucky I am to play music for a living. It brought enlightenment to me at a time when I needed it. To feel that again put me back in a place where I can do it with gratitude.

Britt Lightning: When it's your job, you do forget some of the joy sometimes. Sometimes it's work. You forget that the alternative is that you're a lawyer or someone stuck in an office, looking at papers. It's awakening to see the joy you had when you were a kid in these adults. It's transformative.

Roger Daltrey: It's very easy in this business, where we're bestowed incredible privilege, to forget where you came from. The camp really reminded me of where I was when I played my first guitar. And everyone I know that's done it has had a good time. Guitarists like Jeff Beck come out with enthusiasm. That means something. The passion these campers have for it, it's just liberating.

Rob Halford: When you leave rock camp, you're taking a lot of things with you in your head, and your heart, and your soul. These incredible experiences live with you sometimes for the rest of your life. For many of them, it has been a really life-changing experience. It was for me too. It took me back to when I first started. I wasn't expecting that feeling to come back, but it did. It was just a joy.

Lita Ford: A lot of campers have problems they want to overcome, whether it's with music or in their personal life. They bring it all to the camp. Within those five days, they show their true colors. They work out their anger. They leave here, it's absolutely life-changing. It helps them for the best. One camp, I had a female lead singer who didn't want to sing about rock 'n' roll, didn't want to sing about drugs or sex. I said to her, "What do you want to sing about? What is in you that brought you here? Why did you pay this money to come here if you don't want to sing about these things?" She said, "I'm in agony." I said, "That's a great song title. Let's write a song called 'Agony.'" We wrote this kickass song called "Agony" and she got up and sang the hell out of it. When she first got there, she wouldn't stand up, she was glued to her chair. When we wrote "Agony," she's on stage singing lead vocals to the song. You've got to find what ails them and work through it.

Ed Oates: Leaving the camp, it changed us as a band. We talked about it on the drive back home. What did we learn? We learned we can be a band. We can be more than five guys that just get together to play. It profoundly changed the way our band operates.

Jim Stanard: It was the first time I had performed since the '60s. The significance of the camp to me was that experience. It turned me on.

Kamesh Nagarajan: Music transcends everything.

7

HEY, MA, I COULDA BEEN A ROCK STAR!
(BUT YOU MADE ME GO TO COLLEGE)

Many campers arrive home from camp with new inspiration to pick up their instruments and play. They record albums, form new bands, and reconnect with their love of music. One camper even opened for Aerosmith! That's what it's all about for me—giving people a chance to reignite old passions and find new dreams.

Vinny Apice: It's cool to see someone come from the camp and get more serious about their instrument. The next time you see them, they say, "Here's my demo."

Anthony Mullin: I had met Brad Whitford of Aerosmith a few times, and now I'm at camp playing "Toys in the Attic" with Joe Perry. Later, I noticed one of Aerosmith's managers was there, and I recognized her. We got talking and stayed in touch. When I got back to New York after camp, I noticed Aerosmith released some tour dates for their 2014 Let Rock Rule Tour. In my band, the lead singer is Russian. He's from Moscow. I looked at the tour dates and noticed they were playing in Moscow. I thought, "What if…." I talked to my signer, and through this convoluted set of relationships, we knew someone at a promotion company that was responsible for bringing Aerosmith to Moscow. We brainstormed. I knew Brad, I had just met the management at the camp. Why not propose? I wrote a letter to the management and they let us open for them. Talk about a dream come true. These are the days you live for. We played the Olimpiyskiy Stadium, about 30,000 in attendance. There were no other bands but us and Aerosmith. Just before we went onstage, the lights went dark and the crowd went apeshit. They walked us to a ramp with a flashlight. I saw Brad Whitford and my dad standing there. That was the best way to go on stage. That night, I got a glimpse of what it's like. Rock camp gave me that.

Troy Garrity: Since camp, I've recorded about seventy songs. They're available on iTunes and vinyl.

Amy Edwards: I've recorded, I don't know, four or five albums since then, and I've definitely grown as an artist. My last release was two years ago. I did a double album called *Magic*. I've continued to play and become a songwriter and be accepted in the Austin music community, which is really validating.

Larry Harris: Helena takes guitar lessons now five times a week. We have a vocal coach working with her twice a week. We turned one of the bedrooms into a home studio. She's figuring out how to write her own songs. She's thirteen now. It really was a life-changing experience.

Jim Stanard: Kip Winger was my counselor, and after camp, he ended up being a musical mentor to me, and he became a good friend. I began performing a lot, mostly open mics. I would do about seventy a year. Eventually, Kip said, "Have you ever tried writing songs?" He held my hand and guided me through songwriting technique. I got pretty obsessive about that and started reaching out to other places to learn songwriting. After I had written about twelve songs, Kip said, "Let's make an album." He got me out to Nashville in a recording studio with some great musicians, and part of it we did at his house. That was called *Bucket List*. We were all quite happy with it. It got a handful of good reviews. CD Baby called it the best independent album of the year. I got radio play on 150 stations, college stations. Just when I was doing that, I went to the Nancy Wilson camp. I continued to work with Kip. We now have a second album that is mixed and ready to master. We'll probably release it in the fall. If not for the camp and David, none of this would have happened.

Liam Gowing: I'm currently making a double album of all the songs I've ever written that were any good. I released an album in 2013 as well.

Rey More: The drummer in our band, John Poole, likes producing albums, and we found out that if you declare that all the proceeds of an album will go to charity, most bands will waive royalties. So we started out by doing a Led Zeppelin tribute album. It was eleven songs. I'd record my guitar parts and send them to John. The main bass player was from Paris, France. Of the people that contributed, all but two of them had met each other at rock camp. We produced and released a Led Zeppelin charity album called *Whole Lot of Love*. It goes to a halfway house in Pittsburgh. Then we did a Beatles tribute album for the Feed the Children charity. This is a direct outgrowth of the camps. You pay a lot of money. I say I can claim David Fishof as a dependent on my taxes. But what you get is priceless: a network of friends all over the world that sticks.

Ed Oates: When we finished that camp, my band came back excited to learn songs. Back in the '60s in college, we had a hundred songs in our setlist. We wanted to go back to that. We made a couple of albums. It was a very fascinating process. One of the guys we met at the rock camp, Jeff Foskett, was the musical director for Brian Wilson at the time. He helped us produce our album. I give a lot of the credit to the rock camp. It taught us who we were as a band and how to operate.

Karen Adams: My marriage ended and my boys and I moved to Atlanta, where I pursued voice lessons and had a renaissance of creating art. Now I'm totally focused on my art. I later fell in love with and married my husband of twelve years, who not coincidentally is an amazing musician and songwriter. I sing with my husband at home and at parties, but my sculptures, paintings, and drawings are my priority. Recently, I was commissioned to create a sculpture of Missy Elliott for her music video, "Why I Still Love You," and I made a little cameo appearance at the end.

Frank Pawlak: The latest chapter in my fantasy-camp dream experience is the establishment of the Rock 'n Roll Fantasy Foundation. For years, David has been supportive of a number of philanthropic causes, and for a long time, I have encouraged him to set up a foundation that would bring the magic of the camp to persons less financially fortunate than many of us. With his assistance, a diverse and committed group of rock-camp alumni has come together to serve as members of a board of directors for the new foundation, bearing a banner slogan: "Changing Lives Through Music." We are in the early formative stages of the foundation but are hopeful of making the Rock 'n' Roll Fantasy Camp dream a reality for impoverished and disenfranchised teens and adults whose musical aspirations might have been thwarted by financial limitations or personal tragedy or trauma.

Vaughan Merlyn: The band they put me in had no bass player, so I volunteered to play bass. That was another life-changing event. I haven't given up the guitar, but I became a bass player. I joined a band after the camp, and I still play gigs.

Peter Gatti: I went back to Florida and told my wife that I needed to play live again. I bought a few keyboards and started looking for a simple bar band. One thing led to another, and I started a show called Decades Rewind, a fourteen-piece show with five lead vocalists and over 100 costume changes. I produce it and play keyboards, and in 2017, we played over eighty-seven shows in more than thirty-five states all over the USA. To this day we're still out there playing and entertaining. None of this would have happened if I did not attend the camp.

ENCORE: MY FAVORITE MEMORIES

Naturally, I have a head full of incredible memories to rival even the most avid camper. They range from the hilarious, like the time Lemmy Kilmister of Motörhead wouldn't jam with the campers until I drank a glass of whiskey with him, to the sublime: in my house growing up, it was God and Ginger Baker, in that order, so imagine how I felt to have Ginger come to camp! I was also honored to host Jeff Beck and Tony Iommi, two of the greatest guitar players in the world. Then there was the time CBS Sports Director Bob Fishman came to camp and brought along my childhood idol, Sandy Koufax. Being orthodox myself, his brave refusal to play baseball on the Sabbath meant the world to me.

But, like so many campers, my favorite memories tend to be the ones that happened away from the glare of stardom. I remember people like April Samuels, a drummer who had breast cancer. She came to rock camp and was inspired to start an organization called Breast Cancer Can Stick It! afterward, which has raised close to $300,000 for the cause.

Another breast-cancer survivor who went on to do great things after camp is Laura Roppe. Several years ago, I noticed that the camps tended to be mostly men, and I wanted to bring in more women (as of this writing, we have just produced our first women-only camp). I reached out to Susan G. Komen for the Cure, and they recommended Laura. When she came to camp, Laura was a lawyer who played music on the side and dreamed of being a writer. After she left rock camp, she wrote a book called *Rocking the Pink* about her experience battling breast cancer, and she dedicated a chapter of the book to the camp. She also wrote an album during her treatment, and Billboard ranked her number three on its list of the top fifty uncharted artists in the world. Years later, I asked her about her experience. She said, "David, I left that camp and I decided I'm not going to be a lawyer anymore. I'm going to become a writer because that's what I want to be." Since then, Laura has written twelve books and is an international bestseller on Amazon. Rock camp gave her the freedom, the push, the courage to do it. "I decided that I'm gonna live my life as authentic as these rock stars," she said. "That's what I learned from your camp."

Looking back at the way rock camp has changed so many lives, I realize the ways it has changed my life too. It has forced me to redefine my concept of success. I still worry about the bottom line. I still want to run a successful business. But I have learned that there is something bigger at stake. Helping people is my new bottom line. So, if you've been to rock camp, let me say thank you. And if not, I hope to see you at the next one.

Here's to the next twenty-five years!

ACKNOWLEDGMENTS

There are many people to thank for this book. I want to thank Travis Atria for his work conducting interviews and putting the book together. Big thanks to Roger Daltrey, Eric Sherman, and all the counselors, superstars, and campers who have attended camp. Thanks to Jeff Rowe and Doug Blush for producing *Rock Camp: The Movie*. Lastly, I want to thank Jeff Morris and his beloved late wife Pam for their constant support of Rock 'n' Roll Fantasy Camp over the years. Pam always had the most wonderful smile on her face. The rooms at camp lit up when she was in them, and we will miss her beauty, grace, and presence forever.

CAMPERS CROSS ABBEY ROAD
MAY ★ 2010 ★ LONDON, ENGLAND

ACE FREHLEY OF KISS
INSTRUCTS CAMPERS IN THEIR STUDIOS
NOVEMBER ★ 2009 ★ HOLLYWOOD, CA

ALICE COOPER
GOOFS AROUND WITH CAMPERS AFTER A JAM
FEBRUARY 2013 ✶ LAS VEGAS, NV

BRET MICHAELS OF POISON, A CAMPER &
MICHAEL ANTHONY OF VAN HALEN
FEBRUARY ✶ 2010 ✶ HOLLYWOOD, CA

BRET MICHAELS OF POISON
Q & A WITH CAMPERS
FEBRUARY ★ 2007 ★ HOLLYWOOD ★ CA

ROCK 'n' ROLL
FANTASY CAMP
ROCKCAMP.COM

ROCK 'n' ROLL
FANTASY CAMP
ROCKCAMP.COM

BRIAN WILSON OF THE BEACH BOYS
INSTRUCTS CAMPERS IN THEIR STUDIOS
FEBRUARY ★ 2007 ★ HOLLYWOOD, CA

CAMPERS HAVING FUN
FEBRUARY ★ 2011 ★ BAHAMAS

CAMPERS HAVING FUN!
AT ROCK AND ROLL FANTASY CAMP

DAVID FISHOF FOUNDER OF ROCK AND ROLL FANTASY CAMP & JOE WALSH
OF THE EAGLES, GIVE A Q&A FOR CAMPERS
NOVEMBER 2007 ★ MGM GRAND LAS VEGAS, NV

DAVID FISHOF FOUNDER OF ROCK AND ROLL
FANTASY CAMP & PAUL STANLEY OF KISS
2011 ★ HOLLYWOOD, CA

DEE SNIDER OF TWISTED SISTER
AUTOGRAPHS GUITARS AT ROCK AND ROLL FANTASY CAMP
JUNE ★ 2003 ★ NEW YORK CITY

PRODUCER EDDIE KRAMER
MIXES CAMPERS ORIGINAL SONGS
CAPITOL STUDIOS ★ HOLLYWOOD, CA

A CAMPER LETS LOOSE AT
ROCK AND ROLL FANTASY CAMP
MAY ★ 2012 ★ HOLLYWOOD, CA

GENE SIMMONS OF KISS
INSTRUCTS A CAMPER IN OUR STUDIOS AT MGM GRAND
OCTOBER 2012 ★ LAS VEGAS, NV

GENE SIMMONS OF KISS
WORKING WITH CAMPERS IN OUR STUDIOS AT MGM GRAND
OCTOBER 2012 ★ LAS VEGAS, NV

GEOFF DOWNES OF YES
GIVES A KEYBOARD DEMONSTRATION
JUNE 2013 ★ LAS VEGAS, NV

GEORGE THOROGOOD
ANSWERS A CAMPERS QUESTIONS
FEBRUARY ★ 2005 ★ HOLLYWOOD ★ CA

CAMPERS BASK IN THE GLORY
FEBRUARY ★ 2005 ★ HOLLYWOOD, CA

OUR TV SHOW
SEASON 1

CAMPERS PERFORM LIVE ON STAGE
AT THE HOUSE OF BLUES ON THE SUNSET STRIP
2006 ★ HOLLYWOOD, CA

OUR "IN EAR" STUDIOS AT MGM GRAND LAS VEGAS
OCTOBER 2012 ★ LAS VEGAS, NV

JACK BRUCE OF CREAM
REHEARSES WITH CAMPERS AT ABBEY ROAD STUDIOS
MAY ★ 2010 ★ LONDON, ENGLAND

JACK BRUCE OF CREAM
PERFORMS LIVE WITH CAMPERS
MAY ★ 2010 ★ LONDON, ENGLAND

JACK BRUCE OF CREAM
RECORDS WITH CAMPERS
NOVEMBER 2012 ★ LAS VEGAS, NV

JEFF BECK
JAMS WITH CAMPERS
APRIL 2013 * LAS VEGAS, NV

JEFF "SKUNK" BAXTER OF THE DOOBIE BROTHERS
GIVES A GUITAR CLINIC TO CAMPERS
NOVEMBER 2012 * LAS VEGAS, NV

JEREMY PIVEN
JOINS OUR ROCKERS ON STAGE
AT THE SAG AWARDS AFTER-PARTY
HOLLYWOOD, CA

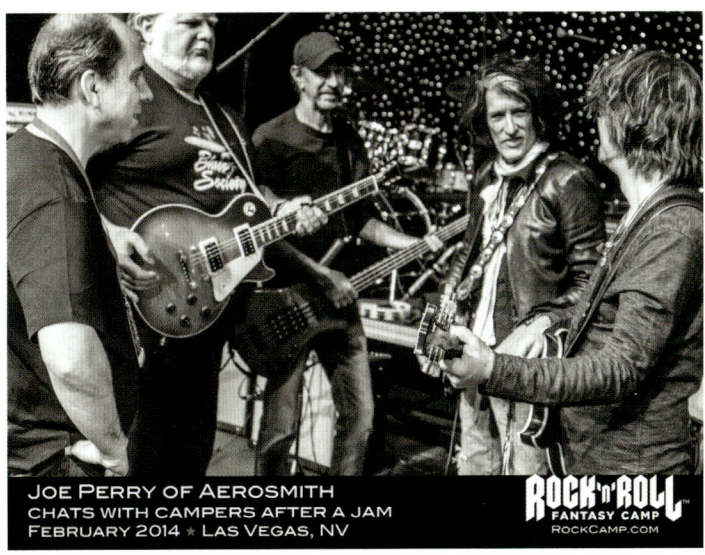

JOE PERRY OF AEROSMITH
CHATS WITH CAMPERS AFTER A JAM
FEBRUARY 2014 ★ LAS VEGAS, NV

JOHN POPPER OF BLUES TRAVELER
JOINS CAMPERS ON STAGE AT MGM GRAND'S ROUGE LOUNGE
NOVEMBER 2012 ★ LAS VEGAS, NV

JOHN WAITE
SIGNS AUTOGRAPHS AT A Q&A
NOVEMBER ★ 2002 ★ HOLLYWOOD, CA

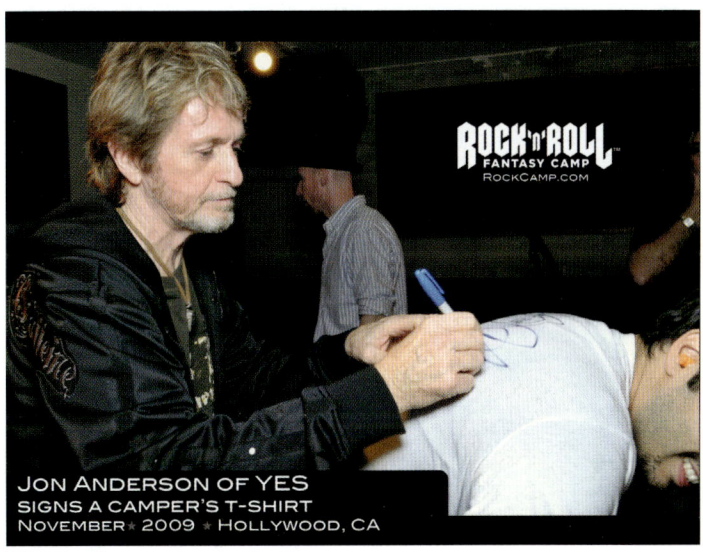

JON ANDERSON OF YES
SIGNS A CAMPER'S T-SHIRT
NOVEMBER ★ 2009 ★ HOLLYWOOD, CA

ROB HALFORD OF JUDAS PRIEST
GETS LOUD WITH A CAMPER
MARCH 2014 ★ LAS VEGAS, NV

SHE SAID "YES"
ON STAGE WITH ROGER DALTREY OF THE WHO
FEBRUARY ★ 2005 ★ HOLLYWOOD, CA

KIP WINGER
ROCKS OUT WITH A CAMPER
AT THE PLAYBOY MANSION
2011 ★ HOLLYWOOD ★ CA

LEMMY KILMISTER OF MOTÖRHEAD
HANGS WITH CAMPERS
FEBRUARY ★ 2011 ★ HOLLYWOOD, CA

LITA FORD OF THE RUNAWAYS & PAUL STANLEY OF KISS
CATCH UP AT OUR PERFORMANCE AT THE PLAYBOY MANSION
2011 ★ HOLLYWOOD, CA

LITA FORD OF THE RUNAWAYS
PERFORMS WITH CAMPERS AT THE PLAYBOY MANSION
2011 ★ HOLLYWOOD, CA

MARQUEE AT THE WHISKY A GO GO
ON THE SUNSET STRIP
FEBRUARY ★ 2012 ★ HOLLYWOOD, CA

A CAMPER GIVES IT HER ALL
at Rock And Roll Fantasy Camp
FEBRUARY ★ 2010 ★ HOLLYWOOD, CA

CAMPER WITH NICKO McBRAIN OF IRON MAIDEN &
ALAN WHITE OF YES
NOVEMBER ★ 2007 ★ LAS VEGAS, NV

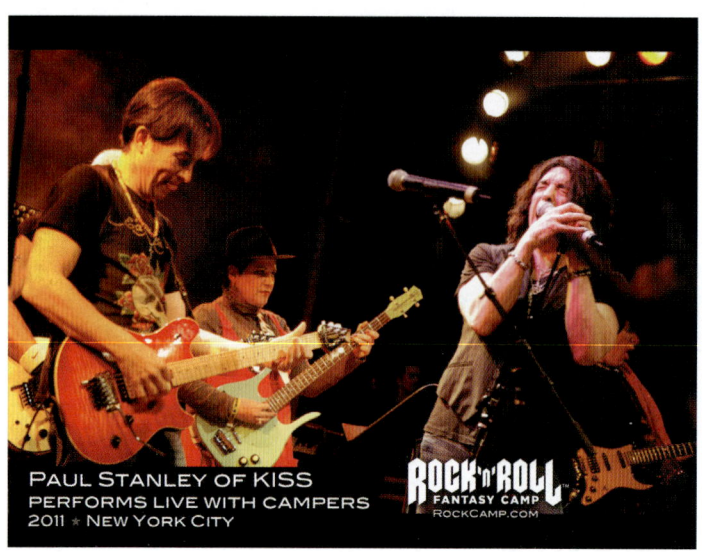

PAUL STANLEY OF KISS
PERFORMS LIVE WITH CAMPERS
2011 ★ NEW YORK CITY

ROCK 'N' ROLL
FANTASY CAMP
ROCKCAMP.COM

RICK NIELSEN OF CHEAP TRICK
JAMS ON STAGE WITH CAMPERS
2006 ★ HOLLYWOOD, CA

ROCK 'N' ROLL
FANTASY CAMP
ROCKCAMP.COM

ROGER DALTREY OF THE WHO
INSTRUCTS A CAMPER
FEBRUARY ★ 2005 ★ HOLLYWOOD ★ CA

ROGER DALTREY OF THE WHO & JOAQUIN PHOENIX
HANG BACKSTAGE AT ROCK AND ROLL FANTASY CAMP
2006 ★ HOLLYWOOD, CA

ROGER DALTREY OF THE WHO
BELTS IT OUT WITH A CAMPER
2006 ★ HOLLYWOOD, CA

SAMMY HAGAR
BELTS IT OUT WITH A CAMPER
MARCH 2013 ★ LAS VEGAS, NV

SAMMY HAGAR OF CHICKENFOOT &
MATT SORUM OF GUNS N' ROSES/VELVET REVOLVER
PERFORM FOR CAMPERS
MAY 2011 ★ HOLLYWOOD, CA

SCOTT IAN OF ANTHRAX
HANGS WITH CAMPERS
FEBRUARY ★ 2010 ★ HOLLYWOOD, CA

CAMPER ROCKS OUT WITH SIMON KIRKE OF BAD COMPANY
★ AUGUST ★ 2011 ★ NEW YORK CITY

SLASH
SCHOOLS A CAMPER
NOVEMBER ★ 2007 ★ LAS VEGAS, NV

SLASH
REHEARSES WITH CAMPERS
NOVEMBER ★ 2007 ★ LAS VEGAS, NV

ROCK 'N' ROLL
FANTASY CAMP
RockCamp.com

ROCK 'N' ROLL
FANTASY CAMP
RockCamp.com

STEVEN ADLER OF GUNS N' ROSES
SIGNS A CAMPER'S DRUMHEAD
2009 ★ HOLLYWOOD, CA

STEVEN TYLER OF AEROSMITH
PERFORMS LIVE ON STAGE WITH CAMPERS
APRIL ★ 2009 ★ HOLLYWOOD, CA

STEVEN TYLER
SINGS WITH A CAMPER
MAY 2012 ★ HOLLYWOOD ★ CA

WARREN HAYNES OF THE ALLMAN BROTHERS BAND
SHOWS CAMPERS GUITAR TECHNIQUES
FEBRUARY 2012 ★ HOLLYWOOD, CA

ROCK 'n' ROLL
FANTASY CAMP
ROCKCAMP.COM